Growing Up on Grosse Ile

Island in the Detroit River

Also by Frances Trix

Europe and the Refugee Crisis: Local Responses to Migrants.
London: I.B. Tauris, 2018.

*Urban Muslim Migrants in Istanbul: Identity and Trauma
among Balkan Immigrants.* London: I.B. Tauris, 2017.

The Sufi Journey of Baba Rexheb. Philadelphia: University
of Pennsylvania Museum of Archaeology and
Anthropology with University of Pennsylvania Press,
2009.

Muslim Voices and Lives in the Contemporary World. Trix,
F. and J. & L. Walbridge (eds.). New York: Palgrave
Macmillan, 2008.

Albanians in Michigan: A Proud People of Southeast Europe.
East Lansing, MI: Michigan State University Press, 2001.

Spiritual Discourse: Learning with an Islamic Master.
Philadelphia: University of Pennsylvania Press, 1993.

This memoir is dedicated to my mother,
Aileen Wilson Trix (1924-2010),
a remarkable woman and a Detroiter
who raised me on the island
and who nourished my love of books and writing.

Growing Up on Grosse Ile

Island in the Detroit River

FRANCES TRIX

Parafine Press
Cleveland, Ohio

First Parafine Press Edition 2020
ISBN:978-1-950843-16-9

Parafine Press
3143 West 33rd Street, Cleveland, Ohio 44109
www.parafinepress.com

Book and cover design by Meredith Pangrace

TABLE OF CONTENTS

PART THREE: Island Life and Landmarks

PART FOUR: High School on the Island and Beyond

PROLOGUE

Growing up on an island means always knowing your boundaries. You can see them. They are not abstract. When you step off you get wet. This is especially true when the island is one that is not citified and not large so that a child can hold the island in its ken.

Grosse Ile fits the bill. It lies at the mouth of the Detroit River far from the city so that the southern end of the island faces Lake Erie. The island itself is nine miles long and two and half miles wide at its widest. There is a canal that goes part way through the island on a diagonal. The north end of the island is called Hennepin Point, after Father Hennepin, a Franciscan who traveled with La Salle through the Great Lakes in 1679. The south end of the island is actually several islands, including Elba Island, Upper Hickory Island, Lower Hickory Island, and Swan Island, that are joined to the main island by small bridges. There was even a sulfurous spring at the south end that we all called "the wonder well."

The name of the island is French—*la Grosse Ile* means "the large island." Indeed it is larger than other islands in the Detroit River. Its native name was *Kitchiminichin*, with the same meaning as the French. It was "purchased" through treaty by the Macomb brothers from twenty-four Potawatomi chiefs in 1776, although we now understand that the Indians thought "the treaty" was meant to be a sign of sharing the island. It was a lush island with many trees, including fruit trees, and the land was flat so there was potential for farming, but it was even better for hunting and fishing. Although the Detroit River became an international boundary between the United States and Canada, Grosse Ile lies closer to the US mainland. Eventually, from the 1870s through much of the 1920s, a train connected the island from the Michigan side; early on it even went across the island to Stony Island, and then by ferry to Canada. In 1913 a private toll bridge was built on the northwest side of the island to connect it to the US mainland. After the train had closed down, in 1931 a second bridge, a county bridge known as "the free bridge," was built where the train had been on the central west side, to further link the island to the US mainland.

There are other islands in the Detroit River, all of which are smaller. Two of these are nonetheless well known. Close to the Canadian side is one whose earlier French name was *Ile aux Bois Blanc* or "White Tree Island," probably in reference to birch trees. The name was somehow Anglicized into "Bob-lo," and for many years housed an amusement park that drew people from the Detroit area and from the city and towns on the Canadian side. The other well-known island in the Detroit River is further north and close to the city of Detroit. It was originally known as *Ile aux Cochons* or "Hog Island," referring to wild pigs. Local residents used this as a commons for their animals. When this was made into a park for the city of Detroit in 1879, people decided its name would have to go. They changed it to "Belle Isle," referring to Isabella Cass, daughter of a prominent Detroit family. But neither of these two islands have long-standing resident communities like Grosse Ile.

In 1763 after the French and Indian Wars when the British took over French lands in the north of North America, the spelling of *la Grosse Ile* on maps was Anglicized to "Grosse Isle." But the islanders, remembering the earlier French name of their island preferred it. Some say it was in the 1850s that the movement for moving back to the French name gained strength; others say it was early in the twentieth century. In any case it was successful and Grosse Ile was finally able to return to its French name, albeit without the article in the front.

What was it like to grow up in a place with such clear boundaries surrounded by water? It was its own understated theater with no need for a separate audience. We knew each other all too well. At the same time, we gave each other room. It was not exactly privacy, but people understood it was not wise to get too close.

When many people in America became concerned with ethnicity in the 1960s, this did not affect the island. Identity was not a concern for islanders. The island itself gave us tangible identity. It had a special quality. We knew this every time we crossed the bridge to come home.

Later I would study and live in different countries and cultures in the Middle East and in the Balkans. The experience of growing up on the island prepared me to appreciate small-town life. I had also become aware early on of contrasts with life on the island and that in Detroit and the social life of a wealthier community on the other side of Detroit through relatives.

In writing about growing up on the island, I came to realize the extent to which we cooperated and were not particularly engaged in conflict or competition. This was reinforced by certain conventions. If people had special experiences or abilities, they often kept them to themselves. In general no one commented. Bragging was deeply frowned on. By the same token people did not complain. They kept to themselves and coped.

On the negative side there could be isolation and loneliness. People dealt with this in different ways. In the mid-twentieth century some people fished, some gardened, some read, and others drank a lot. Women's lives were limited in what they could do. As young people we knew we would have to leave the island for further education and for work. I consider how well island life prepared us for this.

Islands are metaphors for the fragility of life. From the outset islanders knew they had to be careful with the number of trees they cut down for firewood. How they treated the people around them mattered since they might need their help. They were also their social life. Further, they were dependent on the mainland for all manner of supplies. And while the island appeared to surround and protect its young, growing up on an island like Grosse Ile placed a double burden on the young. As they grew, they needed to understand that they would have to move beyond both their family bounds, but also beyond the island, and negotiate life off-island. Their later movement to the mainland was a feature of their island existence.

There are islands all over the world. All islands have similarities, but at the same time, each island has its own culture for each island is related to and contrasts from the mainland around it and has its own history. Grosse Ile is in southeast Michigan in the Detroit River. It draws from old French river culture. It is also a borderland—an international border with Canada that you could walk across on the ice in the winter. I feel at home all along the St. Lawrence Seaway, a long river water borderland with the Great Lakes, past Niagara Falls and Buffalo, up to Montreal, and through to Quebec and the Maritimes.

Growing up on Grosse Ile shaped me and those of my generation on the island. I give perspective on this and share with readers a special place and time. This is the story of growing up on a small Michigan border island in the middle of the twentieth century. The world percolated in, but like the fog horns that blew from the ships as they passed in the night, the sounds were often muted. The river was always with us.

PART ONE:
Early Life
on the Island

Aerial view of Grosse Ile in the Detroit River from the south, as viewed from an aircraft shortly after takeoff from Detroit Metropolitan Airport. Grosse Ile Municipal Airport can be seen at the southern end of the island. Photo by Tim Kiser (TimK MSI).

The Middle of the Island: Pine Needles and Polio

I grew up in the middle of the island. So my earliest memories are not of the river flowing past or even the two bridges that connect the island to the American mainland on one side, or the view of the Canadian shore on the other. My earliest memories are of trees, the tall pine trees that rose above the back of our one-story house, and the pine needles and pine cones that we ran across and threw at each other and always kept under foot. I can still remember the smell of the pines, the scratchy feel of their trunks, and the way they swayed in the wind.

In front of our house there was a mountain ash tree, good for climbing since its branches were low and smooth, and unlike the pines had no sap. But its white flowers when they bloomed smelled awful. There were crabapple trees, and juniper bushes with their special smell and bluish berries by the side of the house.

Our house was at the end of a short gravel road known as Colonial Court. Someone with patriotic thoughts must have named it in the 1930s when they built the houses. Still our house number was 21557.

Why such a long number? There were only five other houses on the dead-end road with ours. This house number would cause me trouble much later when I went to college and the mother of my Connecticut roommate thought I came from a housing project in Detroit due to the long house number. Nor were there anywhere near that many houses on the island. Rather, at some point someone had decided to give numbers to the houses on the island. To make things easier, they had just taken our Edison numbers, that is, our electric bill numbers, and used these as house numbers.

On the corner where Colonial Court met the larger road was the house of H.C.L. Jackson, a person of some renown who wrote for the large city newspaper up the river, *The Detroit News*. One day my sister, who was two years older, walked with me to H.C.L. Jackson's

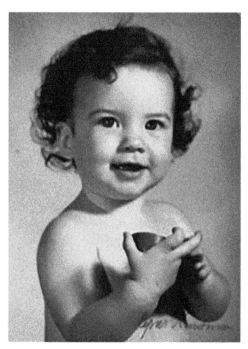

Frances at a young age.
Photo by Cyrus Kinsman,
islander and long the
photographer of islanders.

house. He must have been working on his regular column. Apparently he had a serious conversation with my five-year-old sister and me. I was quoted as contributing the comment, "Green eye." People always thought that my sister and I with our dark hair looked alike but we did not. She had brown eyes and I had green eyes. Later a street on the island would be named for H.C.L. Jackson. And later I would write books. But "green eye" at age three would remain my first published words.

The larger road on the corner was Church Road, which went across the island from west to east at its widest part. It had tall elm trees when I was little that curved up and looked like a church. That was before Dutch elm disease destroyed so many elms in America. But people said the road had been named at a time when there used to be two churches on it, one on each side of the island—a small Protestant gathering place on the west side that did not last and a Catholic one on the east side where it still stands today as St. Anne Chapel. They said that at one time a pastor and a priest rowed over together from the American side on Sundays to serve their two parishes before the bridges were built. But when I was young I did not go out on Church Road.

Instead my mother made us stay around the house at our end of the court. In the summer it was so hot. Air conditioning did not exist and the island was humid in summer. Sometimes it seemed even with fans that the air did not move. My mother made us take naps every afternoon so we would not get sick. The fear was polio. And yet a girl on Church Road who was between the ages of my sister and me did get polio. Even closer, my friend Suzanne's grandfather, Bapu, who lived next door to us, died of polio. It happened suddenly, in two days, and was a neighborhood tragedy. This was before the vaccinations for polio came out.

The Kronks lived on the other side of our house. We would watch Greg Kronk wash the car with a hose. And Whitney Sawyer across the road would wash their car with a hose. Washing cars is something that young men seemed to do. One of my earliest memories is when my mother was on the telephone and I wandered out of the house over to the Sawyers to watch Whitney washing the car. My mother found my pants in the back hall but no child. She eventually traced me to the neighbors. The hose swirled with water from being stored in spirals, and sometimes if we were lucky the water sped out and got everyone who was watching wet. There was a time however when Greg Kronk did not wash their car. I later learned it was the Korean War. He returned and continued washing the car. In contrast, my father had no interest in washing cars.

I learned about the Korean War from my mother, who would send money and write letters every month to a young girl, a Korean war orphan named Kim Jung Ok. Her name stayed in my mind because it was so different. She would write letters back to my mother in Korean. It was a delicate script, like nothing I had ever seen before. There would be a translation included. My mother bought two paintings of Korean art that she hung in our dining room and later one of her favorite pieces of art was a longitudinal green print of classical Korean art that belonged to the DIA, the Detroit Institute of Art. I have it in my bedroom to this day.

Our house backed onto fields and woods on land that all belonged to the Stantons, an old island family.

Some rows of trees had been planted at one time for commercial purposes behind our house, but then let grow out on their own. In the field was a magnificent oak tree just made for climbing. We would climb up that tree and claim perches where we would sit. It even had wild strawberries underneath it.

Beyond the field there were rows of poplar trees and trails. Further yet there was a barn where they kept bales of fertilizer and beside it a place for the killing of chickens. Beyond that there were garden paths with bushes and trees, known as Westcroft Gardens, where people could walk along the paths among beautiful rhododendron and azalea bushes. Mr. Stanton grew rhododendrons and azaleas in nearby greenhouses and sold these commercially. He had hybridized them to grow better in the cold Midwestern climate.

Azaleas in bloom in Westcroft Gardens. Photo by Brian Campbell.

When I was little I was told that Mrs. Stanton, originally Constance Blauvelt, an island girl, had been very beautiful. When the Prince of Wales had come to Detroit early in the twentieth century, he had danced with her twice. But it was Mr. Stanton whom I found more intriguing as a child. I was told that he "had to work outside." It took a while before people explained this to me, and even longer before I truly understood what had happened.

It turned out that Mr. Stanton had driven an ambulance in World War I, and had been gassed. It was because of this that he had to work outside all the rest of his adult life. So he had developed the beautiful Westcroft Gardens with the different colored rhododendrons and azaleas.

The island had seemed so protected and isolated with its own bridges and water on both sides, down river far away from the big city. And yet in my early years polio had come to the island. The Korean War touched us. And much earlier, World War I had come to the island too.

The Milk Truck, Fish and Duck Hunting, Family Talk, and Cinnamon Toast

When we were small, one of our favorite vehicles was the milk truck. It came around regularly on the island in the years before I went to school. The milkman in his uniform on his tall truck brought bottles of milk to our doorstep several days a week. To keep track of how many bottles we needed, and how much we owed, we had a special long milk card. My mother kept it in a drawer in the kitchen next to the back door. It came to be called the "milk card drawer" and all sorts of other important things were kept there too.

Long after milk was no longer delivered by truck on the island and there was no milk card, we still called that drawer the "milk card drawer." When I grew up, in every place I lived, I always had a "milk card drawer." And come to find out, so did my sister and brother.

Our kitchen was a small narrow room, not like the big modern ones. But what my mother said was most important was there was a window over the sink. She could look out as she was washing the dishes. And she could see who was coming down the court. We also had an icebox. Or at least that is what my mother called it. It was really a refrigerator, but Mom was used to the old name, so we all called it an "icebox" too. It lasted over forty years.

The island used to be known for its fish. Before, the river around the island had been teeming with whitefish, and other fish like pickerel and herring. Stony Island, just across from Grosse Ile even had a commercial fishery on it. Boats came up from Ohio to fish our whitefish, and islanders had fishing grounds and sold the fish in Detroit through the nineteenth century. But this was all in the past. A low water year in 1895 finished off the Stony Island Fishery, and when they dredged the channels in the river for bigger ships in 1905, it affected the migration of fish and the fisheries on Grassy Isle and Belle Isle to the north also closed. But what was worse was the pollution that later came down the river from Detroit.

So when I was growing up on the island, we never ate fish from the river around the island. When new people moved to the island, if we liked them, we told them not to eat the fish. If we didn't like them, we didn't tell them anything. For vacations, my father, who liked to fish, would find a lake where we would stay up north in Michigan. We would eat the fish he caught there, but not island fish.

Duck hunting was a common pasttime among men who had grown up on the island. There was a special duck hunting season. To make sure that people did not over hunt, hunters had to have a license and were allowed a bag limit of six ducks. Still people said you could not find some of the earlier species that used to migrate past the island. One father of a student in my class at school was an inveterate duck hunter. He was from an old island family and had married his island wife when she was only sixteen. She would gut and clean his ducks. As he got older, he liked duck hunting so much, he would even stay on some of the small islands in the river where you could find the ducks.

In the past there had been farms on the island with fruit orchards, fields of corn, hay, and wheat, and animals, but by the time I was growing up, there were no longer farms of any size. Still many people had small fruit and vegetable gardens. People had fresh fruit in season, like strawberries, then raspberries and blueberries, pears, plums, and apples, but we did not have the variety of fruit that we have today, even in the stores. For example, fresh oranges were a special treat. If someone went to Florida, they might bring back a few, and an orange could be a Christmas gift. But they were not available in the grocery store.

People tended to overcook vegetables. Apart from corn on the cob, which everyone liked, I wasn't fond of vegetables. My father insisted we clean our plates, but when my mother served vegetables for dinner, they would sit on my plate until the end of the meal. One night I could not stand the lima beans. Everyone else had left the table. I saw my chance and quickly dumped them behind the buffet in the dining room. I had learned this from my sister who had been dumping food there for some time and never got caught. Unfortunately my father saw me. He made my mother cook some more lima beans so I could eat them.

I did not think it was fair. My father hated beets so my mother never cooked them. A few months later I made this point. What we finally decided was that everyone was allowed an amnesty. I had not heard that word before. I learned that while it mostly means "an official pardon," here it meant that everyone had one food they did not have to eat. For my father it was beets; for me, lima beans.

When we were little, we all had trouble pronouncing some of the dishes my mother made regularly. Mom took to calling them what we had called them. A favorite was "tuna mahum bahum." It turned out this was "tuna mushroom casserole." Sometimes when there was company, we would forget and ask Mom to make "tuna mahum bahum." The guest would be totally kerflummoxed.

Another family name for food that we all knew was "cold leftover warmed up." It did not need any explanation. Mom did not talk about that in front of company. After a big meal one night, we knew that the next night what was most likely was "cold leftover warmed up."

Another variation was "hot or cold must go." This was slightly different. This tended to come when Mom had been cleaning the icebox. She would find food that she had forgotten about. Or sometimes she would put things on the electric saw out in the garage to keep cold. She would sometimes forget about them. Then when she remembered, we would need to eat them, "hot or cold must go."

I imagine everyone on the island had family talk like this. I do not know of any special island talk. The closest may be from island food columnist Sid Corbett, who described an island vegetable soup with ten ingredients called "All That's Left." Islanders would make it at the end of the summer with all the leftover vegetables from their gardens.

As for desserts, mothers made pies and cakes, although ice cream was probably the favorite if we were given a choice. But what my mother did best was special food like gingerbread with its wonderful smell, or apple crisp.

Since there were no restaurants on the island, people always ate at home. It would be a big treat to go out for dinner at a restaurant in Detroit. And since the main grocery stores were off-island, you had to be organized in your shopping and preparation. So home-cooked food was more important than it is today.

My mother knew how to make certain foods become almost a ritual. Waffles or pancakes on a Saturday morning with butter and maple syrup were like that. You could savor them as we all gathered around the breakfast table with different parts of the morning newspaper, *The Detroit Free Press*, and my parents had several cups of coffee. And cinnamon toast after church by the fireplace became a special treat in wintertime. Outside it was so cold. But inside, we would all sit in the living room on the floor around the fireplace, and eat hot buttered toast with cinnamon and sugar on it and drink hot tea. There was nothing better.

Hot waffles with butter on Saturday mornings.
Photo by Joan Nagrant, waffles by Lester Johnson.

Mr. Brown's Pharmacy and a Doctor who Made House Calls

The first time I ever saw a round platter full of shelled nuts, high and all lit up, was at Mr. Brown's Pharmacy. They were near the check-out register by the front of the store. To the right was a long mirror and below that were the deep ice cream containers. In front of these was the counter where people sat on the spinning stools and ordered milk shakes and other forbidden items. Across the aisle from the counter and stools was a tall layered shelf, full from top to bottom with candy bars.

The store itself was a narrow one with the pharmacy part in the back. There were shelves along the outer walls and a central section encased with shelves. Up high on the walls and all round the store were historical depictions of "great moments in medicine." You could get lost looking up at these.

When I was little, Mr. Brown's Pharmacy was on the south side of Macomb Street, near the end toward East River Road. It was an old building with steps you had to climb up to get in. Later, Mr. Brown built a new larger pharmacy, across on the other side of Macomb

Street. It had better parking and was on a level, so people could get in more easily. But when I was little, I remember the steps up.

Mr. Brown was the pharmacist. His wife worked there and so did their blond daughter. It was a good business since everyone on the island who needed drugs or basic supplies like bandages or remedies for poison ivy came to Mr. Brown's Pharmacy. It was the only place for such things on the island.

It was a treat for us when we were little to go there with my mother. We liked to walk along the narrow aisles and look up at "great moments in medicine." We would wait while my mother got what she needed.

My most memorable time at Mr. Brown's Pharmacy was when I was very small. I must have come with my mother without my sister. While my mother was waiting to pay up at the cash register, I had stood by the spinning stools with my back to the counter and looked up and down at all the candy bars. They were just my height. I must have reached out and taken one. I don't even remember which kind I took. Then my mother told me to come and we left the store. We walked out and went down the steps.

I got into the car in the back seat when Mr. Brown came out and knocked on the window of the back seat where I was. I looked up. I opened the window. My mother looked back at him. "Did you take something without paying?" asked Mr. Brown.

There I was on the back seat. I crouched down on the floor behind my mother's seat and found a penny. I gave the penny to Mr. Brown. I was mortified. He nodded and went back into the store. My mother did not say anything.

I am not sure if I knew I was stealing. In the past my mother had sometimes bought things for us. But did I know what they cost? No. Did I know that we needed to pay for them with money? I must have since I gave Mr. Brown a penny. I do not remember enjoying whatever I took. I certainly never forgot the experience.

Years later when I had a son of my own, I must have told him about my experience at Mr. Brown's Pharmacy. I certainly told him about "great moments in medicine" all around the high walls of the store. Those depictions stayed with me.

One day when we were living in Family Housing at the University of Michigan, my son, who was about six, was being especially difficult. I took a loaf of pita bread, the kind that are flat and round, and hurled it across the room in frustration. My son looked up at me from his chair at the dining table. He paused and then said, "Great moments in mothering." It was perfect and we both burst out laughing. It brought Mr. Brown's Pharmacy back to me.

As for medical care, many people on the island went to Dr. Lewis. Dr. Lewis lived on the island, but his office was on the second floor of an old building off-island in Wyandotte. I still remember the smell of the stairs as we climbed up to his office. The waiting room always was full of mothers and children. You sat in the plastic-covered chairs and wished you were somewhere else.

Dr. Lewis had a nurse, Miss LaBeau. When it was your turn, you would be called and go into a room. After being checked, the worst time was when Miss LaBeau would come into the room with her hand behind her large back. She always had a shot there.

This was a time when doctors thought shots were the answer for many ailments.

My mother had another answer too. On the way home, we would stop at Affholder Brother's Creamery for an ice cream cone. I think that often helped more than the shot.

We all got the usual childhood ailments: chicken pox, measles, and mumps, and we passed them around. But I think on top of these, we all had allergies too. The island has a high water table. So it was not wise to have a basement in most houses. If you had a basement, it was likely to flood. Nothing smells worse than a flooded basement. I know because I remember when the basement of Andersons' house on Church Road flooded.

But since we did not have a basement, the floorboards in our house molded. We had mildew in our house and in our closets. I got allergies to mold.

What was special though was that Dr. Lewis made house calls. When one of us was really sick, he would come to the house. We took this for granted, not realizing how special it was. Now I see how much you can learn about a patient's situation from seeing where and how they live. But almost no doctor ever goes to a patient's home nowadays.

As for polio, the Salk vaccine came in national use in 1955. They vaccinated all of us on the island at school so no child would be left out. Since then most people have forgotten the fear that had been engendered from the polio epidemic of the early 1950s when many people caught polio in America and many, including our next-door neighbor on the island, died.

Early Attraction to French: Leg Braces to Ballet

One of my earliest memories is walking alone down a long hallway into darkness in an upper floor of the many-storied Fisher Building in Detroit. Far behind me were my mother and an orthopedic doctor. I assume they were watching how I walked. But for me it was the aloneness and the darkness that I recall. I was maybe three.

I was born with what they called pronated hips. My legs turned in. What to do? The doctor prescribed straight metal leg braces that I had to wear at night to turn my legs out. That meant that when I went to the bathroom at night I often fell. My sister remembers me crashing in the night. I also had to have someone do exercises with my legs. My father was recruited to do these in the evening. He would count in German to twenty as he did these. But the foreign language I was most taken with was French.

My grandfather, my father's father, whom I loved deeply, used to greet me in French. "*Bonjour Françoise,*" he would say to me. "*Comment ça va?*" I wanted to be able to answer him. Or he would greet me in Italian, or German, with my name *Franchesca* or *Franciska*. But

I liked French best. I vowed I would learn French so I could answer back to my Grampa. I just liked the sounds of French and I must have had a good ear. Other than my grandfather's greetings and my father's counting in German—he had had to learn chemical German for graduate school—no one else in my family spoke a foreign language. But early on I resolved to learn French and asked for French records to try to do this on my own. I was fortunate that my parents listened to me and for my next birthday they bought me French records. I listened to them again and again until I had memorized them. To this day I remember them. *Allo, passez vingt de quinze. Oui, qui est à l'operet? Ici Pierre. Bernard est là?* People underestimate the memory of young children when they are committed and I truly wanted to respond to my Grandfather.

Of course I repeated other things I heard too. I remember when I was small and my mother took me in the bathroom and washed my mouth out with green soap. I have no recollection of what I had said. No doubt it was something I had heard and that my mother had thought was inappropriate. But all I remember is that Palmolive soap does not taste good. I think my mother thought twice about this too, for she never did it again.

Meanwhile, my walking was not getting any better. I could run and jump and climb trees just fine. But apparently it did not look right to people like my mother. So she kept trying to find ways for me to get my legs more turned out. The next summer she took me to another doctor. This doctor said I should either take ballet lessons or do ice skating. Since it was August, ballet made the most sense. Ballet would help my hips get in line according to this doctor.

So I started at a local ballet school in Wyandotte, a town just off the island. It was frustration from the word go. In ballet there are five basic leg and foot positions. They require you to turn your legs and feet out to the sides at ninety degree angles to your body. My legs and feet turned exactly the opposite way into my body. I could do all five positions backwards, that is, turned inward.

Première, à la seconde, troisième, quatrième, cinquième. But as for the French names of the five positions—I learned these faster than anyone in the class and could pronounce them better than the teacher. I just could not do any of them with my legs and feet.

We all wore little black leotards and stood at the barre. The room was full of mirrors so we could see what we were doing or not doing. *Plié,* and then *balancé.* I learned the arm movements and the rhythm of moving. But never, never would I be able to do the basic leg and feet positions. What had that doctor been thinking? I learned about posture though. For that I am grateful. I got a sense of my body in a different way. And I liked the French names.

Just before kindergarten the doctor decided I should wear tight adhesive straps that wound around my legs, attached to my shoes and went up to a band around my hips. They would work all day at straightening my legs out. I did not say anything the first time these were put on me. I wore them a few times at home. But then, the first day of kindergarten, I tore them off my shoes. I was not going to go to my first day of school with straps wound around my legs. My mother must have understood. She never made me wear them.

Meanwhile my interest in ballet had grown. I would read about it and about great ballet dancers. I knew the paintings by Degas. When I was seven years old, my grandparents got tickets when the Sadler's Wells Ballet came to Detroit. It was the "The Firebird" and Margot Fonteyn was dancing the main role. I leaned forward during the entire performance. It was magical. I had never seen anything so beautiful. I would never be a ballet dancer but I would never forget having seen Margot Fonteyn dance "The Firebird."

Frances at age four in a dress, a rare occurrence.

Later I did ice skate on the Detroit River. I was not a good ice skater. Partly it was because I always got my older sister's skates and they never fit right. My feet were narrower. Skating on the Detroit River was also a true challenge. The ice was never smooth and there were always ridges and snow. I fell a lot. Still it was exciting and fun. Would ice skating have helped straighten out my legs? Maybe if the skates had fit and been tight at my ankles, it might have helped. Who knows. But then I would never have learned about posture and dance movement. The river has no French that I know of. And I would never have seen Margot Fonteyn dance "The Firebird."

Earlier French River Culture, Sugar Bush French

My grandfather had introduced me to French when he greeted me in French. His own father, my great-grandfather, I later learned, had been fluent in French. He had come north from New Orleans after the Civil War as a young man with his mother. His father, originally from Alsace in France, had died of sickness in New Orleans during the war. His mother, of Cajun background, had gone on to Canada where there were still French-speaking communities, but he, John Trix, had stayed on in Detroit.

Much earlier, all along the Detroit River on both sides, north to Lake St. Clair and down to Lake Erie there used to be many French speakers. When Cadillac founded *La Ville d'étroit*, "the City of the Strait," in 1701, he had encouraged settlers. The next year he even brought his own wife. The French had a settlement pattern we call "ribbon farms" since their homesteads were long properties that all had access to the river. This made sense because the river was the highway for travel and transport.

The French had first come as explorers and fur traders in the 1600s. They recognized that they needed to work with the different Indian tribes in the area. Catholic priests also came with the French. When the French began to settle in the 1700s to stabilize the region and the fur trade against British competition, some of the French married Indian women, while others brought French wives from Montreal or France. The resulting French culture in places like Detroit was a frontier culture, but one with good food based on French wheat, Indian corn, and Great Lakes fish and other foods of the region.

So when people recall the Thanksgiving meal of the Pilgrims in New England, in French Detroit, the harvest feasts were much better. For one thing we had vineyards and there was even a fall festival known as the "Festival of the Grape." The grapes were ripe by this time and pressed in the old way of stomping on them and then being blessed by the priest. People put out long tables. On them they had bread baked from French wheat, fresh fish from the river, grilled, and still hot. There were vegetables from the gardens of the *habitants*, the French settlers, along with jams and jellies they had made the previous year. For meat, there would be a ham, waterfowl, and a turkey. But the main meat was venison brought by the local Indians, either freshly killed, or smoked or dried. Of course this all was served with red wine from earlier years.

When the British took over Detroit from the French in 1763, they did not show respect to the Indians the way the French had. The Indians resented this and Pontiac, a leader of Ottawas, even led a siege of Detroit that almost succeeded. With the American Revolutionary War in the East, no one was upset to think of the British leaving, although the British hung on to Detroit until

History Detroit

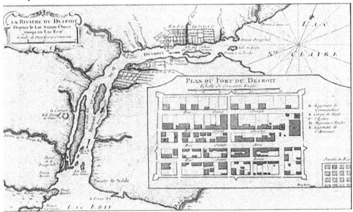

1763 Detroit From Bellin's 1764 Atlas

The Detroit River showing Grosse Ile at end of French Control of the Region.

1794. At this time the people of Detroit were two-thirds French. The French culture persisted.

Father Gabriel Richard of France came to Detroit in 1798. There was a fire that destroyed the entire city of Detroit in 1805. After the fire, Father Richard wrote what became the motto of the city of Detroit in Latin that translates, "We hope for better things; it will arise from the ashes." Father Richard brought the first printing press to the city in 1809. A Protestant church even asked him to be their pastor. When the first regularly published newspaper was printed in Detroit in 1817, the *Detroit Gazette,* it was printed in French and English. That same year Father Richard was one of the founders in Detroit of what became the University of Michigan. Father Richard was elected as a delegate from the Michigan Territory to the US House of Representatives from 1823-1825. He died in

1832 helping cholera victims and is respected to this day as one of Detroit's great leaders.

To what extent was Grosse Ile affected by French river culture? Certainly the island has a French name and it was under the French flag for many decades. Father Hennepin described the fruit trees of the island in his journal so it appears he landed there in 1679. Indian and French river cultures were the cultures of the region in the 17th and 18th centuries and on into the beginning of the nineteenth century. However when the island was divided for property, it was not done according to the French system, but according to the British system. This happened because it was done rather late after the Macomb brothers "purchased" it in 1776. They were not from the region but were from Ireland via northern New York State. The island was not surveyed until 1808 and 1819.

The two Macomb brothers married French women. Alexander Macomb married Catherine Navarre and they had eleven children, of whom eight were born in Detroit. William Macomb married Sarah Jane Dring, who was of Huguenot background, a family that had moved from France to England. They had eleven children, all born in Detroit. One of their children, William Macomb II, married Monique Navarre, and brought her to live in his home on the island that was on East River Road south of Horsemill Road.

In the War of 1812, William Macomb II was captured by the British and taken to Montreal. Monique was left on the island where she gave birth to a son. At the christening of the baby, three weeks later, Indians raided their house and set fire to it. There is a story that William had had a sweetheart among the Fox

Indians and when she heard he had married a French woman, she had drowned herself. In revenge the Indians decided to destroy William's house. Somehow Monique escaped with the baby. She made it across the canal, by boat to the mainland, and walked all the way to Detroit, almost twenty miles, carrying her son. Once she got there, she died of exposure, but her son, Navarre, survived and lived to a good age. On his return from Montreal, her husband rebuilt the house and married another French woman, Jeanette Marentete. They had eight children.

Over time in the nineteenth century on the island, people took to living in the same pattern as the ribbon farms, so that each household had access to the river. Further, people on the island were affected to a certain extent by what went on in Detroit where French culture was still alive through the first half of the nineteenth century, and by culture across the border in Windsor, where they often found priests, or in Amherstburg directly across the border from the island where they shopped.

As for French families on the island, the two best known are the Reaumes and the Bouchers. There is historical evidence that Louis Reaume bought land on the island in 1831. Louis Reaume and his wife Charlotte Latout had eighteen children, all born in what is now Windsor, Canada. But most of their children came to Grosse Ile where they married and had children. Louis Reaume sold some of his land on the island in 1832 to Charles Boucher. He had married Julie Lavalée on a return trip to Montreal and they had twelve children, many of whom came to Grosse Ile.

The Reaumes and Bouchers had similar histories.

Both families had come originally from France, gone to Montreal, and come to Detroit in the time of Cadillac. A Reaume ancestor had actually led the wife of Cadillac from Montreal to Detroit in 1702. And this wife was related to the Bouchers.

I went to school on the island with Reaumes and Bouchers, but also with other classmates with French names like Forshee, Payette, Mousseau, and Ouellette. Since early settlers had married French women, it is impossible to tell what other islanders also have French roots just by their names.

Another aspect of French river culture on the island is the Catholic Church. There had been visiting priests to Grosse Ile ever since Jeanette Marentete had married William Macomb II in 1816.

The granddaughters of Jeanette Marentete, a Mrs. Brodhead and a Mrs. Wendell, continued to house the priest when he visited, as had their grandmother. After the Civil War, the priest had taken to coming to the Brodhead house on East River Road on a Saturday. He would come from across the river, either by canoe, or on foot on the ice in winter, from Assumption Parish in Windsor. A Black servant of the Brodheads would go around the island in a horse-drawn cart to let the other Catholics know the priest had arrived. They would all come for confession and some would stay nearby for the night. On Sunday the priest would say mass and there would be a potluck meal. Then the priest would return across the river.

From these times, funds were slowly gathered for a Catholic church. Protestants contributed as well, as had Catholics for the earlier Protestant church. Land was donated in 1768 at the corner of East River Road and Church Road. Finally in 1871 St. Anne's Church was dedicated, named like the first Catholic Church in Detroit from 1701.

The French language survives as a spoken language only in areas around Windsor on the Canadian side of the Detroit River. In Windsor itself, and especially in Detroit, many street names reflect the earlier French heritage. In Detroit I currently live on Orleans Street, near St. Aubin, Chene, Rivard, and Dequindre. Main streets in Detroit include Beaubien and Livernois. All of these except Orleans are from names of French families that had ribbon farms in the area. There are also cities along the river, north of Detroit with French heritage and names like Grosse Pointe, or south of Detroit with French heritage and names like Ecorse and River Rouge.

There is even historical evidence of how French was spoken in the Detroit region. It comes from lists of words that early French speakers made, paired with Native Indian words, mostly of Chippewa languages. They were trying to document the Indian languages, but at the same time, they also documented their French speech of the time. Some were just to pair meanings, but others had grammatical forms and sound patterns too, thereby giving a more complete view of their French speech. This was a time when people were not doing dialect studies of major western languages. So these lists became valuable as early evidence of a French dialect study. The speech became known as "Sugar Bush Speech," or Detroit French Dialect, largely a Norman-based dialect. My earliest publication when I was hired at Wayne State University was to write a glossary of the linguistic terms of Sugar Bush French for a French-Canadian journal so readers who were not linguists could understand it. The French became less formally known on the Michigan side as "Muskrat French," since Catholics in southeast Michigan had a dispensation to eat muskrat on Fridays.

Returning to the question as to whether French river culture affected the island, I think features of French river culture and island culture overlap. Certainly in the past, French river culture was one of the cultures of the region. It was a culture of survival and fitting in with local people. It valued cultivation of the land, hunting the waterfowl, and fishing the river. People did not seek to stand out. Children did what their parents had done. Island culture has these values as well. People help each other, but at the same time, they are independent if possible. There is no point in competition or division. On the island, Catholics helped the Protestants and the Protestants aided the Catholics in their fundraising, and later in getting stones from Stony Island for the building of the Catholic church. They even had a joint Sunday school at one time before the churches were built, and joint bazaars and socials.

I have traveled up to Montreal and Quebec City in Quebec. I feel comfortable there. I do not know if it is because these cities are on a large river and I love to be by big rivers. Or is the French culture part of the reason I feel at home? I cannot separate the physical setting from the culture.

Motor City, Ford, Percherons, and Islands in the Great Lakes

Before I went to kindergarten, I knew my first name began with an "F." When I was four, my sister had started writing in first grade. She wrote out the first letter of my name for me. But I had seen that letter before on billboards and on signs outside dealerships on the way to our grandparents. It was the first letter of "Ford." Later when I started to do cursive writing in second grade, I would write the first letter of my first name the same way Ford did on their vehicles. There were Fords all over, including on the island.

Of the main automobile companies—General Motors, Chrysler, American Motors, and Ford—all had their headquarters in Detroit except for Ford. Ford had their world headquarters in Dearborn closer to the island.

It was during the heyday of the 1920s that the Motor City got its reputation as a major industrial center and as "the Paris of the Midwest." Both my grandfathers, who were mechanical engineers, worked in Detroit at this time. The Detroit Institute of Arts, with is magnificent collections, and the main Detroit Public Library Building were both completed in the 1920s. Both are Renaissance style in white marble and stand across from each other on Woodward Avenue in Midtown Detroit. This was also the time when the handsome tall buildings in downtown were constructed. But the only effect on the island was that some prominent people built impressive estates. Ransom Olds, who founded the Olds Motor Vehicle Company that would become Oldsmobile of General Motors, had a magnificent estate built on Elba Island in 1916. It became the largest house on the island and served as a summer home for Mr. Olds.

I became curious why Detroit had become the Motor City. Between 1901 and 1908, there were over 500 companies formed in the United States for making automobiles and most of them failed. There were people developing automobiles all around the Upper Midwest. Cleveland, Ohio, or Gary, Indiana, could have become a center of automobile manufacture. Why did Detroit become the center?

What was needed was capital and people willing to invest it, a pool of skilled workers, and inventors with good ideas. Detroit had capital and people willing to invest from the earlier timber trade in Michigan. But so did several other cities. As for skilled workers, Detroit had been a center of stove manufacture and had skilled workers, but so did other cities. There needed to be inventors with good ideas. Detroit certainly had these, but they were also found in other cities. What appeared to have distinguished Detroit was that in Detroit the inventors built on each other's ideas to a greater extent so they went forward faster.

As for Henry Ford, he grew up on a farm in Dearborn, and failed in business multiple times until he was forty years old. In 1903 he began production of the Model A which finally succeeded. The assembly line was the result of multiple influences and experimentation. It was implemented for Ford's Model T in the Highland Park Plant in 1913 and increased productivity. Ford announced his famous $5 a day wage in 1914, along with decreasing work hours from nine to eight hours per day, and increasing shifts from two to three so work was continuous. The context for these changes was low morale at the Highland Park plant, absenteeism, and turnover. The workers had not liked the assembly line work and there had been communication problems with the change in workers from the earlier ones to the more recent immigrant populations. The hope was that with higher wages and shorter hours, they would have better living conditions, and be more loyal and disciplined in their work. It was also hoped that workers would be able to purchase automobiles.

None of this affected the island directly. We did not even have a bridge until 1913, and so automobiles were not a factor in life on the island. The main way to the island was through the ferry service from Trenton to the island. That is why Ferry Road had its name. The west end of Ferry Road was where there used to be a ferry that connected the island to Trenton across the river. It was said that getting onto the ferry from the island dock was easy, but the Trenton side had an embankment. If you had a horse and carriage, it was hard to get down the embankment and onto the dock before you got onto the ferry. In winter there was no ferry. And there had not always been a ferry service. The road used to be called "Lime Kiln Road." Its name was changed in the middle of the nineteenth century when ferry service started. Before then people had to get to the island by private boat or by lake steamboat. For a while at the end of the nineteenth century, steamboats would stop on the east side of the island and take people to the mainland. In the summer they would take people to Sugar Island amusement park and stop on the way to and from at the island. But when the park closed so did the boat service.

A Mr. Voigt was the one who built the Toll Bridge. He had a brewery in Detroit and kept Percheron horses, on a farm on the north end of the island, that pulled his brewery wagons. He wanted to be able to get his draft horses off and on the island more easily so he built the Toll Bridge in 1913. There is a story in my family about this kind of horse. When my mother and her younger sister were playing in a piano recital, her father said to his wife, "Don't our daughters play like a pair of young Percherons." My mother said she did not know what this meant until later in life.

Even with the Toll Bridge the population of the island was still low. The census of 1920 listed only 802 people. With the second bridge in the 1930s, automobiles became more common. The population of the island grew. More professional people moved to the island after World War II, including people who worked for Ford Motor Company in Dearborn. Options for Ford professionals were to live in west Dearborn, or in Grosse Pointe, east of Detroit, which was a much longer commute, or on the island. Grosse Ile was a short commute, only twenty minutes to Dearborn. We knew people who worked in management for the Ford Motor Company who lived on the island.

The automobile changed the city of Detroit, and not in positive ways. Detroit used to have very good public transportation with streetcars that went up and down Jefferson and Woodward Avenues every three minutes. My mother used to take these to school. People did not need automobiles then. They could just hop on the streetcar and get to work or shopping. But the automobile companies wanted people to buy cars, so with the government sponsored highway systems in the 1950s, not only were city neighborhoods destroyed, but the streetcars were sold to Mexico City in 1956. There were buses but they were not anywhere as good as the streetcars had been. People needed automobiles then. And the highways went right through the poorer neighborhoods of Black Bottom (named for the quality of its soil) which had become the Black neighborhood of Hastings Street on the east side, and Corktown on the west side. Parking lots were needed and took over where old homes had been. My great-grandfather's house in Midtown was destroyed for the Cancer Center parking lot.

Not all places were in favor of motorized vehicles. The most famous island in the Great Lakes does not even allow them. That is Mackinac Island up north in Lake Huron just to the east of the Mackinac Straits. The ban on motorized vehicles has been in effect on Mackinac Island since 1898 when they were said to have scared the horses. Most of the island is a state park—the first Michigan State Park. Travel is by foot, bicycle, horse and carriage, or roller skate and roller-blade. You have to take a ferry to get to the island. It is the major tourist destination in Michigan and has a remarkable hotel, the Grand Hotel, that looks out on

Lake Huron. What I also remember about Mackinac Island, besides the hiking, is the chocolate.

Nearby to the north in Lake Huron is Drummond Island. It is the biggest island in the Great Lakes. Most of it is owned by the State of Michigan. There are many tourist activities to engage in on the island—hiking, golf, fishing, and boating. The full-time residents are only about 1,000. Mostly people come in the summer.

Another famous island in the Great Lakes of Michigan is Isle Royale in Lake Superior. It too is a park—Isle Royale National Park. It is far north and the top soil is thin. There are no roads on the island and the only wheeled vehicles that are allowed are wheelchairs, and the occasional jeep or tractor for safety personal. It has no permanent residents, but many hiking trails. It is accessible by ferries and seaplanes.

Yet another large island in the Great Lakes of Michigan is Beaver Island in northern Lake Michigan near Charlevoix. It has a colorful history, first with an offshoot of Mormons, then with an Irish community in the nineteenth century. Its economy was built on farming, fishing, then timber. These all declined. Since 1970 tourism has come. There are fewer than 700 permanent residents. It can be reached by ferry or air.

Of the main Michigan islands in the Great Lakes—Mackinac Island, Drummond Island, Isle Royale, and Beaver Island, and Grosse Ile—none have significant permanent populations, except Grosse Ile. When I was growing up there were around 7,000 people living on the island. In the census of 2000, there were 10,894 people. Where the other islands have major parks and tourism, Grosse Ile does not. For a time it was a place for wealthy Detroiters to have summer homes or cottages, but this time has passed.

Indeed the automobile is important for the island in the sense that without it, there would not be so many people living on Grosse Ile now. The twentieth century saw a major increase in population, largely because people could live on the island and with the bridges, commute daily to work in the larger Detroit metropolitan area. Before the automobile, people were limited in where they could work. With only horse and boat travel, people could work in Wyandotte or Trenton at most, or they would have to board in Detroit, and just come to the island on weekends.

I am proud of the acumen of Detroiters in developing automobiles and the organizations that manufactured them. They brought hundreds of thousands of people work and changed the way people live. However I wish more care had been taken with our cities, including Detroit, in preserving our neighborhoods. We are now realizing that the highways destroyed much. We are even hoping to fill in some highways so there can be more walking space where some of the old neighborhoods used to be.

The island did not suffer from the highways. Since it was so out of the way, no one ever considered putting a highway through it. There are advantages to being far off center. It didn't hurt that it was an island too. However its roads could use improvement.

Telephone Calling,
Poison Ivy, a Good Neighbor

When I was little, before I went to school, I remember that if you wanted to call someone on the telephone, you had to first talk to the operator. You had to tell the operator the number, and then the operator would connect you. But this terrified me. I could not see the operator. I did not know who she was. How could I talk with her? My mother also mentioned something about "party lines," but I never understood that.

This all kept me from calling my friend Sally Robinson who lived on Church Road across from Colonial Court. I would want to go to visit her, but I did not know if she was home. "Just call and see if they are home," my mother would say. I could not face talking with the operator. Or I would want Sally to come and visit me. "Just call and ask her to come over," my mother would say. Again, it was too much for me.

Until one day when I was four I vowed I would invite my friend over. The telephone was in the hallway by the front door where you could see out the window of the door. I got up my courage and reached up to the telephone. In a small voice when the operator asked,

I gave her the number. She could not hear me. Again I said the number. "Louder please," said the operator. Again I gave her the number. Finally it sounded as if the call was going through. I was so relieved. I looked out the window.

There was Sally, almost at our back door! How could she have heard that I was calling her before the call went through? I put down the phone. She must have guessed that I wanted to see her. That was the first and last time I tried to talk with the operator. After that, telephones changed and you no longer needed to talk with the operator. They figured out a way so that you could dial the numbers yourself! What an improvement. I remember the exchange on the island was OR-6 for Orleans, and then the four-digit number. But I wondered where the operators went.

My other friend when I was little was Suzanne. Suzanne's mother and my mother were friends so we had known each other since we were six months old. She lived farther away than Sally. But her grandmother was Mamu who lived right next door to us. Suzanne was at her grandmother's a lot so that is where I could walk over to see her.

Mamu had a redbud tree and a maple tree in her front yard. These were not good climbing trees. So Suzanne would come over to our house and especially to the sand pile. It was behind our house and just out from the tall pine trees in the sun. It was a good-sized pile of sand. If it had not rained in a while, the sand could be dry. Then we would bring out jars of water from our house to help shape our sand castles and build roadways across the pile. Near the sand pile there were stands of a common flower known as

Queen Anne's Lace. We played for hours in the sand.

Beyond the flowers were bushes in the shade that included some poison ivy. We knew how to recognize it from the three-pronged leaves and the reddish veins in the leaves. We avoided those bushes and my sister and I never got poison ivy on the island, but my friend Suzanne did. She must have been more sensitive. When this happened, Suzanne would go to Mamu, who would put pink calomine lotion on the itchy places.

I liked to be with Suzanne at Mamu's house. It was peaceful. Mamu would sit in her chair in the living room, smoking Kool cigarettes, and we would sit on the sofa. Our feet could not touch the floor yet.

Mamu was thin and had her dark hair rolled inward, all around on top of her head. No one else wore her hair like this on the island. Later I learned it was an old French style from before the 1920s. Mamu was from Vermont and her family came from Quebec. She and her husband Bapu had come to the island when their children were in school. They had built their house on Colonial Court in the 1930s. She kept her house very neat. Her grandson, Stephen, would mow her lawn and she would give him a root beer float. She was a good cook. We all especially remember her brownies. She had a small dog, a dachshund named Frizl.

Once when she was cleaning the bathroom, she had put her wedding ring on the sink. Somehow it got knocked off and fell into the toilet. She called the plumber immediately. He came. It must have gone down deep into the pipes. He dug down and found the ring right on the edge of the septic tank. Thank goodness he found it.

Later I even spent a Christmas at Mamu's. My parents had invited a young German friend named Helmut to stay with us at Christmas, but he had arrived with a wife, so they got my bedroom and I was sent to stay at Mamu's for the holiday. It was a quiet holiday. I remember the wallpaper in Mamu's guest bedroom. It was green leaves and ivy all over the walls.

I went back on Christmas morning to our house to open gifts. We opened Great-grandmother's box after breakfast first. The Germans thought it was an American custom, but we did it because we knew it would be fun. Great-grandmother was living in a home and you never knew what she would send. That year she sent a box of half-eaten chocolates, some suppositories, and a feather duster for my younger brother. Truly the Germans were perplexed.

Later still when Suzanne's family moved to Milwaukee for her father's work, Suzanne stayed behind to finish her senior year of high school on the island. She lived with her grandmother, who let her drive her dark green 1965 Mustang to school. That was truly special. Mamu was quietly there for her and for the rest of us on Colonial Court all my growing up. She was truly a good neighbor.

Nursery School, "Old Maid," Bus Driver Clyde, and Death

When we were little, no one had ever heard of pre-school. Young children like my older sister stayed at home and eventually went to kindergarten. But in the middle of the twentieth century things were changing. One family on the island, the Findleys, decided to start a nursery school. A neighbor's son went so I ended up going with him two mornings a week. I have very little recollection of what we did at nursery school. I do recall that the Findleys lived on the other side of the island and had the nursery school in their home. They had forsythia—yellow flowers by the side of their house. They also had one son who was between the ages of my sister and me.

The one memory of nursery school that I do have was a spring memory. We all came home one day with a bandage on our forearms. When our mothers took off the bandage, it said "April fool" in red ink!

Most island children did not go to nursery school. Rather early learning on the island took place as it always had at home and depended on whatever families brought to their offspring. My mother was one of seven children and she had grown up in Detroit near Belle Isle. Her older sisters had taught her much of what she knew. She passed this on to my sister and me and later to my younger brother. She always had classical music playing in the house as she did the housework. I remember Schubert's "The Trout" especially as she made the beds in the back of the house. I would play the same music for my son when he was small. When she ironed, she listened to classical music on the radio station from the city of Windsor across the river in Canada. I can still hear the Canadian Broadcasting Company call—"This is CBC in Windsor."

My mother read to us in the evening before bed. Her sisters had done that for her as well. She read us all the *Winnie the Pooh* books and older books like *The Tales of King Arthur* and *The Wonder Clock* that had stories of villagers and kings, and wars and adventures where people died. This was before we had television, and even after we had it, there was not much on it. Written stories mattered a lot.

Actually the first people in the neighborhood to get a television were the Hascalls. I remember going over to their house to see it for the first time. We all crowded around the large box. The screen projected in black and white. The first program we ever saw was *Kukla, Fran and Ollie*. Kukla and Ollie were puppets and Fran was the human who spoke directly. I remember that it did not make much sense to me. I think you needed to watch it regularly and we only saw part of it once. It was a program designed for children but more adults watched it. Maybe it was the novelty of it. We did not get a television set in our house until several years later.

Sometimes on afternoons when it was too hot to play outside my mother would play cards with my sister and me, trying to teach us how to lose. I remember one game called "Old Maid." The idea was not to be stuck with the card called "the old maid." Neither of us understood what "the old maid" stood for. We all knew Miss Agnew who worked as a secretary, and lived on Church Road where she took care of her elderly parents. She had never married, but was an islander and respected for herself. As for the card game, my sister and I figured out that all we had to do when one of us got the old maid card was distract Mom and then quickly sit on it. At the end of the game no one had the card. My mother would look at us and wonder. We would smile. No one lost.

But mostly we played outside in the fields and trees. We would go outside in the morning and come home for lunch. I remember when I went to kindergarten it was the first time I had seen playground equipment—metal swings and jungle gyms all on asphalt so when we fell we got bruised and scraped.

When it was time for kindergarten, the big question was whether it would be morning kindergarten or afternoon kindergarten. On the island there was the added complication of how to get the young children to and from the school that was by East River Road, part way down the island. The island itself was long and there were a limited number of buses so this was a complex logistical question, what with getting all the students of the other grades to and from school as well.

We all rode the yellow school buses. That was a special treat for five-year olds. It was not easy to get up the high steps of those big buses. The bus drivers were special people. I especially remember the bus driver my kindergarten year. I used to sit up front and recite poetry to him. He did not seem to mind.

His name was Clyde Lawler. He had a son by the same name. There was great sadness with Mr. Lawler. His first son had been in the basement of his house on Macomb Street in the middle of the island where he had been playing with his father's rifle. He had shot and killed himself. Clyde and his wife had adopted another son whom they also named Clyde. But it cannot have been the same.

Mr. Lawler was kind to all the children. I think I learned about what had happened to his first son by listening to my mother talking on the telephone. In any case I would recite poems to him that I had learned on the long trips home, especially along West River Road. I could recite all of the "Puffin Poem" along that stretch of road.

There once was a puffin, just the shape of a muffin.
He lived on an island in the deep blue sea.
He ate little fishes that were most delicious.
He had them for supper and he had them for tea.

But this poor little puffin he couldn't do nothing
For he hadn't anybody to play with at all.
So he sat on his island and he cried for a while
And he felt very lonely and he felt very small.

Then along came the fishes and said if you wishes
You can have us for playmates instead of for tea.
So now they all play together in all sorts of weather
And the puffin eats pancakes like you and like me.

By the time I finished it was my stop at the end of Church Road. It was a long walk up to the corner of Church Road and Colonial Court, and then down to my house. I had never seen a puffin. I figured Mr. Lawler, who was a hunter, knew ducks so maybe he knew puffins too. I would walk up slowly back to my house, thinking about his son who had shot himself. I would pass the Robinsons' house. Mrs. Robinson had had a little baby boy who died too.

Years later, even the Findleys, the family that had made the first nursery school on the island, learned the sad news of the death of their only son. So they went into their garage next to the forsythia bushes, closed the door and turned on the gas.

Life and death on the island were not far apart.

PART TWO:

Early to Middle Schooling on the Island

Island Life: No One Chose the Sidewalk Books

We did not have a movie theater on the island. If you wanted to go to the movies, your family had to go off-island to Wyandotte or Trenton or into Detroit. But when I was little, islanders did not go to the movies very much. I was surprised when I went away to college to learn about people my age who had gone to the movies every Saturday.

We did not have a library either. But there was a library in the basement of the fire station across the river in Trenton. What a wonderful place for a library. We all loved going there. And across from the fire station was an A&W. Fast food did not exist then, but A&W was the closest we had. After going to the library my mother would sometimes let us stop there for root beer.

We did not need movies or libraries since the island itself was a remarkable place. In summer we played along the west shore in the muck with snails and crayfish, while in winter ice flows cluttered on top of the water. Or we could go to the east side of the island where the river was broad and the current was faster. There we loved to watch the long Great Lakes freighters riding through the different channels. We would listen for their horns as the freighters greeted each other, and watch the buoys swing on the water. Later when I was in college in a landlocked place, I found myself especially homesick one night. What was going on? Then I figured it out. The metal bars on the ropes of the flagpole were clanging and they sounded like the buoys on the river.

Even in our bathtub when we were little, we called the taps Duluth, for the port at the far northwestern end of Lake Superior; and the other end, Cleveland. My sister and I would be freighters as we pushed past each other in the tight channel of the tub, mimicking the path of the freighters on the Great Lakes.

Apart from Macomb Street and Meridian, the other roads on the island were all crowned—people drove down the middle of the roads and people walked there too. Our school buses drove down the middle of the roads, especially in winter, for fear they would slide into the river.

Macomb Street, named after the Macomb Brothers who "bought" the island from the Indians, was the only street on the island with stores. When I was little there was Mr. Brown's Pharmacy, a gas station, and a small food store on Macomb Street. There was one other commercial place called "Four Corners"—where Parkway, the street that came from the Free Bridge crossed Meridian—the road that went along the length of the island. It had another gas station, another small store, and a hair salon where some of our teachers got their hair done. For grocery shopping our mothers had to go off-island.

For most island children, going to Macomb or Four Corners was not something they did. Our parents did not encourage it. And if we wanted to walk to Mr. Brown's Pharmacy to buy a candy bar, I remember it was two and a half miles from our house. So when people on the radio talked about "walking to the corner pharmacy," it would have been a long walk on the muddy or dusty side of the road. The only sidewalks on the island were on Macomb Street.

We played outside in the fields and woods and trees, or by the river or canal. We went to the public school where many of the teachers were islanders. Catholic children went to kindergarten with us at the public school, to the Catholic school on the island from first grade through eighth grade, and then rejoined us in the public school for high school. Those of us in the public school throughout envied those in Catholic school who got extra days off for saints' days. We weren't so sure about their uniforms, though.

After a year of half-day kindergarten, I looked forward to first grade. My teacher's name was Mrs. Penglase. I liked that name. But the first day of class she passed out very strange books. They had only a few words on each page and very simple looking children named Dick and Jane and Sally who did not seem able to talk. They only played on sidewalks. I quickly went through the whole book. I looked up at Mrs. Penglase confused. What was this? She explained it was something called "phonics" and she wrote it on the blackboard. I shuddered.

I let my eyes go down to the desk. As Mrs. Penglase talked about phonics, I looked outside. The elementary school had a very fine playground, better than the kindergarten. I would focus on recess.

I knew what real books looked like. My mother read to us at night from books like *King Arthur and the Knights of the Round Table, The Wonder Clock,* and *The Song of Roland.* These had woodcuts in them, and *Roland* even had one colored print of "the madness of Roland" before he was killed. We were drawn to this print.

Children who grew up outside and in small towns like the island knew about life and death. Our dog Gretel had died giving birth, as had Mrs. O'Connor who lived at the bend in East River Road. Mrs. Robinson who lived down the street had a baby boy who died, and Bapu, our next-door neighbor, Mamu's husband, caught acute polio and tragically died two days later in the early 1950s. On hot summer days when everyone kept the windows open, we could hear people yelling sometimes, and there were people who drank a lot. We knew who these people were, but we would never say their names. It was their business. People on the island had to live with each other.

What Mrs. Penglase had handed out to us did not stand up to the life we knew or the books I knew for a minute. She went on about "sounding out." Who could be bothered with children who could not talk, and who were stupid enough to play on sidewalks where when you fell down you would get scraped. They were not even stories.

When I got to second grade it was with great relief that I found out my teacher was Mrs. Nankervis, a tall islander. She announced that she did not believe in phonics. And what is more, she let us choose the books we wanted from those in the back of the room. No one chose the "sidewalk books."

The summer after second grade I went outside one hot day and told my mother I was bored. My mother was sitting on a chair under some pine trees rocking my baby brother in an old carriage. They did not have strollers then. She looked up at me and said, "With all the books in the world, there is never any reason to be bored." I immediately went inside to the den and began reading my father's childhood books. These were old books, stories about soldiers and wars in times past. Perhaps that is why my life has continued to be full of adventure to this day.

In our stockings for Christmas we always got books. One Christmas when I was in junior high, I got *War and Peace* and did not talk to anyone during the whole holiday.

I may have grown up on a narrow island in the Detroit River, but thanks to my mother and island sense, it was one open to the world of books and to life.

Painting the Sky and River without Blue

When I was in first grade I had art lessons once a week after school with Mrs. Hascall, our neighbor who was also an artist. My kindergarten teacher, Mrs. Walker, had noticed the year before that I did not draw like my fellow classmates. Perhaps it came from helping my mother with Metropolitan Miniatures.

Metropolitan Miniatures were classical paintings and other works of art that came every month in the mail from the Metropolitan Museum of Art in New York City in the form of stamps, like the green stamps we used to get in the grocery store in Wyandotte for discounts. When I was four, my mother had me put the Metropolitan Miniature stamps in the right places in the booklets that also came. So I grew familiar with great works of western classical art, mostly paintings but also sculptures. By the time I began to draw, I had seen images of great works of art and had licked the backs of them and stuck them into booklets for many months. This must have affected how I drew. My ducks did look like ducks. Mrs. Walker even put one of my drawings up on the wall of the school near the office. I think it irritated my sister. My teacher told my mother that I should have art lessons.

And so one day when I was five, I was sent across our gravel court to meet with Mrs. Hascall about art lessons. I already knew the Hascalls as neighbors. The Hascalls had three children that they had adopted all at once. It was the 1950s and people wanted to have three children. But that cannot have been easy. At night I could hear commotion from their house from my bedroom window. Mr. Hascall was an engineer at Ford Motor Company and had studied at Michigan Tech in the Upper Peninsula of Michigan and Mrs. Hascall was an artist. She was an angular woman with a narrow face and big brown eyes.

Mrs. Hascall told me to go out on the screened-in porch and sit down at the table by myself. She gave me paper and pencil. Then she brought out two old cowboy boots. She dumped them on the table on top of each other and told me, "Draw them." They were so ugly. I drew. I do not remember what happened after that except eventually I got art lessons with Mrs. Hascall. It was good that my friend Suzanne joined me for the weekly lessons so they were more fun.

We had our lessons in a side room of the Hascalls' house. We painted in water colors from black and white photographs that Mrs. Hascall had collected, or vases of flowers. I was glad I never saw the cowboy boots again. I liked the paints, their names, and drawing. But I never liked going to Mrs. Hascall's house. It did not feel good to me. I could not have told you why. I was never at ease there.

For the last art lesson of the year, as a special treat, Mrs. Hascall took us to paint outside. Suzanne and I sat on the O'Donnells' lawn, up from East River Road that ran along the river in front of us. Mrs. Hascall, stood off to the side smoking. We looked out across the narrow road to the river and the outline of the Canadian shore far across on the other side of the river. We each had a shoe box of tubes of water color paints and brushes, a plate to put the paints on, and a jar of water to mix our brushes in.

Suzanne and I had been taking weekly art lessons together for well over a year. We both had dark braids but Suzanne's mother was better at braiding than mine. By afternoon, my hair was coming out of the braids. I couldn't have cared less. It was afternoon, the sun was shining, and we were outside by the river for painting.

As I started putting dabs of paint around the edge of my plate—Hooker's Deep Green, Burnt Siena, Payne's Grey, Alizarin Crimson, Lemon Yellow—I noticed that I had no blue. No Cerulean Blue, no Ultramarine, and no Prussian Blue. What was this? How could I have no blue? I loved the names of the paint colors and I especially loved the blues. Mrs. Hascall did not like Prussian Blue. She said it was not a true color. Suzanne and I disagreed but we did not say so to her, and we used it a lot so it made sense that it was gone. But where were the other blues? I must have used them up and Suzanne had too. It was the end of the year.

I looked out at the river. How could I paint the river? At the edge it was a murky color. I could get away without blue there. But then I looked up at the sky? How could I do the sky without blue? I did not say anything. It was my own fault I had no blue left.

Mrs. Hascall came beside us and knelt down. I always liked the different shoes she wore. As she finished her cigarette she asked about what we saw. People in those times smoked a lot and no one noticed. Suzanne said she would paint some green-filled landscape close at hand. That is how she would get away with having no blue. I looked out at the river. We lived in the middle of the island but I was drawn to the river. There was a tree on the nearby shore. At least it was not blue. I told Mrs. Hascall I would paint the tree. She liked that idea. And the grass around it too, I added. Yes. And the far shoreline across the river.

The problem with watercolor is that you have to cover the whole paper with water and do the background first. That meant I would have to deal with the sky and river early on.

But before that I needed to sketch what I would be painting. I looked again at the tree. It was by itself and its branches loped down from the top. The trunk was not straight but curved in different ways. I was growing to like this tree. I sketched it and the grass around its base. In the background I lined the far shore of Canada. It would be a simple painting. The tree was what I would work on. As I was drawing I even forgot about the lack of blue for a while. I forgot about Suzanne and Mrs. Hascall too. That is the joy of art. You forget about other things and just are.

Mrs. Hascall came by and said she thought I was ready to start painting. I covered the special textured watercolor paper with water with my thick brush. I took another look at the sky and river. There was no help there. It never occurred to me to mix colors to make blue. Back to my plate with what colors I had. I went ahead and when I was done, the sky came out a soft green, the river a light yellow. It did look as if there were clouds in the green sky. I painted the far shore of Canada a light brownish green to show it was distant. That worked and contrasted with the yellow river. Then I did the grass in front by the tree. That was mostly brown and grey.

As the background dried, I could work on the tree itself. I climbed trees and knew them well. I painted the trunk in the darker colors I had. I worked on the branches to make them hang down over the yellow water. I had the most fun with the bark of the trunk.

Mrs. Hascall came by and stopped. She looked surprised. Then she did something she should not have. She added a few lighter branches to one side from my branches. I could not have done that. It was my painting, not hers. It was good though. She told me to sign my name in the grass by the shoreline on the right. I had just started learning cursive writing in school. The painting was better than the signature.

The following fall when there was an art show at St. James Church on the island, Mrs. Hascall told me to bring my painting of the tree with the green sky. It was the best painting I ever did, and no blue in it, still my favorite color.

Suzanne and I painted together with Mrs. Hascall for a few more years. My favorite time was when were finishing the lesson and we had to clean our plates. I would mix all the colors in patterns with my fingers as I slowly washed the plate. I remember Mrs. Hascall would also be cooking dinner. She said if the food for dinner had contrasting colors it was well balanced. That made sense to me.

But slowly I realized that I had come to paint like Mrs. Hascall. Not as expertly, but the style was hers, not mine. Something was wrong. So I stopped. And through the years, I never learned to paint people. Always landscapes were what I did best. It is what I loved from growing up outside on the island. People were another matter, best left to themselves, although there was actually not much privacy on the island.

Much later, after the Hascalls had moved to another part of the island to a beautiful house along the river, I visited Mrs. Hascall there. I had long stopped taking art lessons. Their children had grown up and moved away and Mrs. Hascall was traveling and painting overseas and living more what seemed like an artist's life. When I mentioned how lovely her home was she said to me that I had told her, long ago, that her house near ours in the middle of the island did not look like the house of an artist. And so they had moved.

I had no recollection of that. I had not liked how it felt in that house, it was true. And it had not seemed like the house of an artist. But had I said that? She had remembered it. I had no right to say such a thing.

When I graduated from high school, Mrs. Hascall gave me a small oval wooden table. I have it to this day. It fits next to my work chair and I cherish it. On the island, relationships were deeper than we realized.

Frances with braids in early elementary school.

The Most Beautiful Shell and Betrayal

Students from all grades in the island school gathered in the old gymnasium for the program. We younger ones walked from our elementary school, a fairly new one-story building, across an asphalt playground to the old stone former high school. It had fire chutes from the second floor that you had to slide down. We all looked forward to upper grades so we could slide down those fire escapes some day.

I was seven and had never been in the old school building before, let alone the gymnasium. It was big and dark when we got there. Since we were the youngest students, we had to sit on the floor. It smelled of floor polish and gym shoes. How many islanders had played basketball, volleyball, and kickball there over the years?

It was a treat that we younger students were allowed to come so we were told we had to behave. The high windows had ribboned metal on them and strange canvas blinds to make it dark. The basketball nets were raised, hanging high above us at both ends of the gym. To the front was the stage with its thick curtains. The principal of the high school stood on the stage to introduce the visiting speaker. He was an expert on oceans and sea animals.

Since we lived on an island in the Detroit River, we knew snails, turtles, crabs, crayfish, and fresh water critter. But what the man spoke of was another category altogether. We did not have beaches but rather shores of rock, muck, and seaweed. What he showed us were reefs of coral of amazing colors. Truly another world.

He also had shells, all sorts of shells of different shapes and sizes. At one point he held up a shell that took my breath away. He held it carefully in both hands. It was rounded, about the size of a small baseball mitt, but spiraled in an elegant way. It had a pearl light that glistened softly in the dark gym. I had never seen anything so beautiful.

"This is a chambered nautilus," the man said. I do not remember what else he said about the shell. I just stared up at it from my place on the floor. Then he added. "There is a poem about this shell by Oliver Wendell Holmes. Does anyone know this poem?" No one said anything. "That is a pity. If any student knew the poem, I would have given the student the chambered nautilus."

My eyes grew big. I knew what I would do. The speaker left, but no matter. If he ever came back I would be ready.

That night at home I had to find that poem. This was before the internet. And there was no library on the island. I had to find the poem. I went behind the big chair in the living room to where my parents kept a series of books called *The Wonder Book*, a sort of encyclopedia. If the poem was anywhere in our house, it would be there.

My mother must have helped me. I would not have known how to spell Holmes. She said something about him being a doctor in Massachusetts. It turned out his son had become a famous Supreme Court Justice. I did not care. I just cared about the poem and I found it.

I curled back behind the big chair on the floor and read the poem, "The Chambered Nautilus," by Oliver Wendell Holmes. It was published in 1858 and had five stanzas. I did not understand all the words, including a word in the first line. It began:

This is the ship of pearl, which poets feign,
Sails the unshadowed main,
The venturous bark that flings
On the sweet summer wind its purpled wings
In gulfs enchanted, where the Siren sings,
And coral reefs lie bare,
Where the cold sea-maids rise to sun their streaming hair.

And on to the second stanza:

Its webs of living gauze no more unfurl;
Wrecked is the ship of pearl!
And every chambered cell,
Where its dim dreaming life was wont to dwell,
As the frail tenant shaped his growing shell,
Before thee lies revealed,
Its irised ceiling rent, its sunless crypt unsealed!

I learned these lines, crouched on the carpet by the heating vent and the other *World Book* volumes. In my mind was the shell. I especially liked the wording, "the ship of pearl." That made sense to me.

The third stanza was one of work for the sea animal in the shell.

Year after year beheld the silent toil
That spread his lustrous coil;
Still, as the spiral grew,
He left the past year's dwelling for the new,
Stole with soft step its shining archway through,
Built up its idle door,
Stretched in his last-found home, and knew the old no more.

And then the fourth stanza, a sad one, told of a message that the shell would bring.

Thanks for the heavenly message brought by thee,
Child of the wandering sea,
Cast from her lap, forlorn!
From thy dead lips a clearer note is born
Than ever Triton blew from wreathed horn!
While on mine ear it rings,
Through the deep caves of thought I hear a voice that sings:

The last verse ended with the message. I always liked the ending. But I will save that for later.

I have no idea how long I sat there behind the chair reading and memorizing. I learned "The Chambered Nautilus" cold. Some people have said that memorizing is not valuable, that we should be taught to think and analyze, but memorizing is good too. Then we have poems with us for keeps. I had never learned a poem that long before.

I knew the Lord's Prayer. I knew a lot of Christmas carols. But those we recited or sang so much it was not work to learn them. At summer camp we would learn many songs too, but with singing again and again, it is easy to learn many verses. Poetry is different. But it seemed to be out of favor. People did not recite it much. Only later in life when I got to the Middle East did I find cultures that still valued knowing poetry. At home no one mentioned "The Chambered Nautilus," and to be honest, I forgot about it too.

Fortunately in fifth grade my class did go to the old school building where we got to go down the fire chute. At fire drill time we would line up in our classes on the second floor. Then one by one, each of us would sit down and stretch out our legs into the chute. The teacher would tell us to spread our legs to slow us down, but we would bring our legs together to go faster. We would zoom down the chute, popping out at the bottom.

We were baby-boomers so they had to build another school for us for sixth grade. The second part of the year we were in a new building that reminded us of our earlier elementary school. It was one story and light-colored. To our surprise, the man who had come when we were in second grade to talk about oceans and sea animals came back again.

This time we were not in the old gymnasium but in a new multi-purpose room with glass windows. The curtains did not close well. We sat on chairs, not on the floor, and only first through sixth graders came, not all the island students as before. As sixth graders we were the oldest group this time.

The principal introduced the man and he showed the same pictures of reefs and coral. He had the same shells. I waited. Then he held up the chambered nautilus in both hands. It was as beautiful as ever. He went through the same spiel and then asked, "Does anyone know the poem, 'The Chambered Nautilus" by Oliver Wendell Holmes?"

As a tall sixth grader I was sitting in the back. I raised my hand. He looked at me. He nodded slowly, not sure. So I stood up and began.

This is the ship of pearl, which poets feign,
Sails the unshadowed main,
The venturous bark that flings
On the sweet summer wind its purpled wings
In gulfs enchanted, where the Siren sings,
And coral reefs lie bare,
Where the cold sea-maids rise to sun their streaming hair.

"Just go to the last stanza," he said hurriedly. So I went to the end, the fifth and last stanza.

Build thee more stately mansions, O my soul,
As the swift seasons roll!
Leave thy low-vaulted past!
Let each new temple, nobler than the last,
Shut thee from heaven with a dome more vast,
Till thou at length art free,
Leaving thine outgrown shell by life's unresting sea!

Then I sat down. There was silence. My fellow classmates did not know what to make of it. The man told me to see him afterwards. He continued his talk. I was pleased that I had remembered. I had learned the poem four years earlier when I was in second grade. I must have learned it well.

After his talk, I made my way to the back of the multi-purpose room. There the man handed me two angel-wings. Simple white shells that you could hold in one hand. I looked at him. What was this? He had already put the chambered nautilus away in its box. He had no intention of giving it away. I looked at him again. There was nothing to say.

A teacher wanted me to take the shells around to classrooms to show what I had been given for knowing the poem. Did no one remember what had been promised earlier? I refused.

When I went home that day I told my parents what had happened. I have no idea what became of the wings. (My brother remembered that they ended up in the curio table in our living room; after that, no one knows.) But the poem "The Chambered Nautilus" has stayed with me throughout my life and I am well into my sixties now.

Sometimes I say it to myself and wonder how a poem learned at age seven lasts so long. I have come to believe that knowing the poem is more valuable than having the shell. Although the shell was of consummate beauty.

A chambered nautilus.
Photo by F. Trix

Detroit's Bicentennial, Prohibition, Downriver, and the Ambassador Bridge

When important things happened like fireworks over the Detroit River in early July, or Christmas parades on Thanksgiving Day, they happened downtown in the city of Detroit. In July it was a joint combination of American Independence Day (July 4) with Canada's Dominion Day (July 1) in fireworks over the Detroit River. As for the Christmas parade, it too was impressive as it came up Woodward Avenue, Detroit's main street, and was supported by the J.L. Hudson Company, Detroit's main department store for many decades.

My grandfather told me about Detroit's bicentennial. Since Detroit was founded in 1701, its bicentennial was in 1901. To begin the festivities, a man dressed in green velvet like Cadillac was supposed to step off a boat at the foot of the city to commemorate its founding. Only by accident he stepped off the boat into the water. Then there were floats that started to come up Woodward Avenue. But they got stuck on the streetcar tracks. The final event was an evening one. Young maidens dressed in white gathered together on a barge. When they began singing, the barge was sent out in the Detroit River past Belle Isle. It was truly a lovely sight. But then the barge got caught in the current. They hadn't figured out how to bring it back in. It was a scramble with boats going out trying to bring the maidens back in. After all this, my grandfather said he did not ever need another bicentennial.

As for Grosse Ile, it had at most three brushes with fame. The first was when the French first came to settle the area in 1701. It was said they had considered building their settlement on the island, but fearing they might run out of firewood, they had sailed back up the river and built it instead on a slight promontory on the narrowest part of the river. The river itself was a strait between Lake Huron and Lake Erie—hence the French name, *La Ville d'étroit,* "The City of the strait" —which became Detroit.

The only problem with this is that the French founders of Detroit came from the north through Ontario, Lake Huron, and down Lake St. Clair to the river. So they found the narrow place along the river for their settlement first. A story about going further south down the river to the island with twenty-five canoes and then deciding there would not be enough firewood is hardly credible. The only evidence of this is a French legend.

The second alleged brush with fame was in the nineteenth century when the Underground Railroad brought escaped slaves up from the South through Michigan to Canada. Some were said to have gone across by boat to the island and then across the Detroit River to Canada. There is even a river house that was supposed to have been a haven for them on the island.

However Isabella Swan, the island historian, could find no evidence of this. Certainly it made better sense to cross by Detroit where the river is much narrower.

The third brush with fame was during Prohibition from 1918 to 1933. The Detroit River would freeze over in the winter and people would drive cars to Canada from the island and come back with their cars packed with alcohol. This makes the most sense since the island was far from authorities. It is said the bottom of the Detroit River is covered with bottles from this time.

Most people on the island however were content to let world events take place far away. The island was sufficient to them, although they depended deeply on the other downriver communities around them.

In the late nineteenth century, when there were fewer people in the different downriver towns, there were Saturday night dances in the summer that drew young people from Ecorse, Trenton, and Amherstburg to Grosse Ile. Everyone came by boat. These built on regular connections. East side islanders used to buy food in Amherstburg in Canada. West side islanders and others took the ferry across to Trenton. Islanders bought hardware and drugs in Trenton. The only doctors were in Wyandotte.

There continue to be connections of the island with other downriver communities and this is not surprising. Islands, unless they are very large, always depend on the mainland around them. When I was growing up, we went to Trenton for Mulias and Elias Department Store that my mother affectionately called "mules and elephants." It was a good store and you could find whatever you wanted there. It was tragic for the whole area when it later burned down in 1987.

We also went to Elizabeth Park in Trenton where the ice in the skating rinks was smooth, unlike the ice on the river. Once the police were called to Elizabeth Park for an alleged meeting of the Ku Klux Klan. It turned out it was the Latin Club from Grosse Ile that was having an end of year meeting, all in white togas. We went to Riverview to Louie's for gas. And we went to Wyandotte weekly for groceries and for the doctor and dentist. My father also worked at Wyandotte Chemicals. Today the hospital is in Wyandotte as are other necessities. The good public library is in Trenton. Mainlanders have their boats at Grosse Ile boat clubs, including the Elba-Mar Boat Club, and the Ford Boat Club. The connections continue.

But in elementary school things were more restricted. As young people we knew everyone on the island but we did not know young people on the mainland. Still the textbooks did come from somewhere else.

In third grade a new subject appeared. It was called "social studies." The world was trying to come to the island through our textbooks whether we wanted it or not. In the social studies books we read, "Canada is north of the United States." The problem with this was that we all knew that Canada was due east of the island. We saw it every day across the shipping lanes of the river. No one put much store in social studies after that. The writing in the books was lifeless and there were no stories which did not help.

In third grade Miss Rimes tried to have us write poetry. Maybe it was due to her name, "Rimes." I had always liked to learn poems, but I had not written them before. Unfortunately Miss Rimes did not give us good examples or seem to have a sense that good poetry needed feelings. That might have helped. I think all we produced was doggerel, mindless rhymes.

Later when I was at the university another teacher tried to have us produce short poems for an English class. In this situation we had been inundated with great poems. It was almost too much. I had reverted to my island memories.

There had been a man who had lived with nature somewhere on the northeast shore of the island. He spent his time walking the roads of the island. We called him "Mr. Kick-a-Stone" because it seemed that was all he did. His name was Din Rooney. So I wrote on him. I do not think Miss Rimes would have liked what I wrote, but the professor had. It was before they cleaned up the pollution in the river.

Din Rooney
Din Rooney drank river water.
Thick after-city water,
Color of the sky water,
Goose-turd green.

Third grade was also the year of Easter bonnets. For Easter that year Miss Rimes had us make Easter hats out of paper plates and crepe paper. It was not exciting but it was fun to play with the crepe paper. I made a paper plate hat with cerulean blue crepe paper all around it, blue still being my favorite color, and one pink flower on it. It was simple and I thought very fine. Other students put many colors on theirs. Miss Rimes chose my hat and one by another girl, Diana Witt, that had purple, yellow, and orange, all in a mountain of color.

Our hats could not have been more different. Miss Rimes had the two of us wear our hats into the fourth grade where the fourth graders would vote on which one they liked the best. No one voted for my hat. I was mortified. I went home and told my mother and cried. I cannot remember what my mother said. I had a different aesthetic than my classmates. That is hard for a third grader.

As I think back, I think it was my love of the Ambassador Bridge that made me like simple lines. The Ambassador Bridge is a long suspension bridge over the Detroit River, connecting Detroit and Windsor. When I first saw it I was smitten. The simple lines are so elegant. When it was built in 1929, it was the longest suspension bridge in the world. I saw it every time my family drove from the island through Detroit, along Jefferson Avenue, over old cobblestone streets in the warehouse district, on past the east side of Detroit to visit my grandparents. My grandparents were both raised in Detroit. My grandfather's family home had been taken over by the city in midtown so he had moved further east to Grosse Pointe. We visited them fairly often since my father was an only child and he was a good son. But my father had moved the other direction downriver to try to spare my mother the difficulty of living too close to his own mother who was judgmental and critical of her.

Even today, many years later, where I now live in downtown Detroit I can look out my window and see the simple sweeping lines of the Ambassador Bridge. They will be building a new bridge soon. They will name it the Gordie Howe Bridge after the great Canadian hockey player who played for the Detroit

Red Wings. But the lines in the drawings are not as elegant as those of the Ambassador Bridge. As for hats, they are mostly out of fashion. But if I were to buy one, it would still be a simple one like the one I made in third grade.

The Ambassador Bridge connecting Detroit and Windsor across the Detroit River. Photo by F. Trix

First Spelling Bee on the Island and Camp in Canada

In fourth grade we had Mrs. McCall. She had us rush up to the blackboard in rows to do multiplication tables. We enjoyed that. But it was clear she was having a rough year herself. On the island no one talked about personal problems, but we all knew when things were not right. She would stand, hold her head, and send us out to recess, a wise solution. We knew we were a good class so it had to be something personal she was dealing with. We loved recess so it suited us. I remember especially the milkweed beside the recess area. It grew all along the fields there. Milkweed are not so plentiful now and are crucial to Monarch butterflies that are endangered. But then we just liked to play with the fluff and the milky goo of the milkweed.

That was also the year of the spelling bee. We were not a competitive lot. We tended to work together. So when Cynthia Davies had trouble with Iceland during a quiz, I leaned back and gave her "Reykjavik," and she leaned forward and gave me "plateau." The teacher had not minded.

It was the principal's idea, a Mr. Rohrer, to have a spelling bee. He was not an islander. We were given lists of words to practice and then came the day of the spelling bee. Almost all the fourth graders decided to participate. We had never had a spelling bee before.

It was held in the cafeteria and was going fairly well, we thought, although people tended to help each other. Mr. Rohrer had to remind us not to do that. Then Mr. Rohrer said "hygiene."

That seemed strange to us. Billy Langdon did the best he could. "Hi Jean" he said, and spelled: "h-i J-e-a-n." "Wrong," said the principal. What was wrong with it? The next student tried, "h-i G-e-n-e," as in Gene Autry. "Wrong" said the principal again. This was not going so well. Our whole line of fourth graders did some variation of Billy's "h i J-e-a-n." "Sit down," said the principal, but none of us sat down.

"Hygiene," said the principal. He raised his chin as he spelled—"h-y-g-i-e-n-e." What an ugly spelling, I thought.

"Hygiene means health," added the principal.

The fourth graders did not move. None of us believed him. And what is more, it had not been on our list of words. Why would you need an extra word for health?

It was a standoff.

Finally the principal looked over at the other fourth-grade teacher. She looked down. Then she said, "I think it is time for lunch. All go back to your rooms and pick up your lunch bags."

And that was the end of our first spelling bee on the island.

It was after fourth grade that I went to camp in Canada for the first time. My grandparents had Canadian friends who owned a whiskey company across the river, east of Windsor, and had asked them for a recommendation for a summer camp in Canada. They suggested the Taylor-Statten camps north of Toronto in Algonquin Park. These are the oldest continuously running camps in Canada. Canadian Prime Minister Pierre Trudeau, and later his son, Justin Trudeau, who also became Prime Minister, went to them. Canadians take camp seriously. We did not know this of course. It was just where my sister and I were being sent for the month of July.

Dressed in our grey blazers, our trunks loaded with the long list of required items, including the heavy sleeping bags people had then, we stood outside the train station in the evening in the Windsor train station, saying goodbye to our parents. I was nine years old and my sister was eleven. It was scary. We slept that night on the train and got to Toronto in the morning. There we met many other campers. We somehow got on another train that headed north, past Lake Simcoe, up toward Algonquin Park. They got us onto buses and then to boats to take us part way across Canoe Lake to the girls' camp, Wapomeo, which was an island in Canoe Lake. That was the last I saw of my sister for a month.

We were all assigned cabins of seven girls each. Our trunks fit under our beds. Walking down to the cabins I could smell the outhouses. It was dark from the trees and you had to watch out for roots of trees or risk tripping. But the boulders that made up the sides of the island were large and soothing. Precambrian I later learned. It was an old topography. The first morning they tested our swimming abilities. I was not a good swimmer. Many people on Grosse Ile did not swim because of the pollution. So I had to wear a red scarf around my neck showing that I could not swim twenty-five yards. It was degrading. I soon managed to do twenty-five yards of dog paddle so I could take off the scarf. But I would never learn the crawl. Something about the breathing eluded me. Side-stroke came easier.

What I really came to like was canoeing. Paddling low on the water from the side of the canoe felt just right to me. I liked the j-stroke to keep the canoe in a straight line. I also painted my paddle with a large green dragon that I could see with each stroke. Other people put little designs on their paddles. No one else filled the whole paddle the way I did, let alone with a wavy green dragon, big and bold with spikes on his back and a red tongue and teeth.

Every morning we got up and went skinny dipping in the lake. Then we came back, dressed, and had breakfast. After breakfast we would sing "O Canada" by the flag. On Sundays, we also sang "God Save the Queen." There was always porridge for breakfast. I grew to like this hearty oatmeal. In the evening after dinner there was singing. That is where I learned to sing about the ship *Titanic*. I had never heard of the *Titanic*. I memorized all the songs. It was healthy living.

I was the only American in my cabin. All the others were Canadian. I sensed it was wise not to stand out. My accent was not strong. I had grown up on the border and had listened to CBC in Windsor for years. Later, when people would ask my sister or me where we were from, we learned to say, "West of Amherstburg." Amherstburg is south of Windsor and across the ship channels from Grosse Ile, so we were being truthful. But since their geography was as weak as that of most Americans, they did not figure out that we were from Michigan.

We went on a canoe trip for several days with the whole cabin, our counselors, and a male guide. It rained of course and the tent was not truly waterproof. The bread got hard and had to be cut with an axe.

At the end of the month, we went back the way we had come. My sister did not want to go back home. She was happier at camp than she had been on Grosse Ile. I liked both places, but I loved the canoeing and the large boulders around the shore. Both my sister and I would return to Wapomeo for three more summers, and my brother would go to Ahmek, the boys' camp. I was grateful for the experience. Whether you call it hygiene or not, this truly made us healthier.

When I paddled a canoe, gliding along low in the water, I was reminded that canoeing was how the native peoples had traveled around Grosse Ile and the Detroit River in earlier days before the French came in 1701, and even after they came until the British took over and then the Americans. Camping in Algonquin Park took ingenuity and planning. The north country was not that different from Michigan in frontier days. It was canoeing that made me happiest. Or as the canoeing song goes:

My paddle's keen and bright,
Flashing with silver.
Follow the wild goose flight,
Dip, dip and swing.

Dip, dip and swing her back,
Flashing with silver.
Follow the wild goose flight,
Dip, dip and swing.

Boats and the Great Lakes to Great Lakes Freighters

People no longer paddled canoes by the island as they had in earlier times, but there were still boats lying beside people's houses, in garages, or in the water by docks. Before the bridges were built, boats were crucial for islanders. But after the bridges came, boats were more for pleasure. Two of the main wharves became yacht clubs. There was one on the west side of the island by the Free Bridge that had cruisers and outboards, and one on the north side of Upper Hickory Island at the southeast end of Grosse Ile. It had many sailboats and powerboats too. This was closer to Lake Erie. There was even a third smaller boat club by Elba Island. What people preferred though was to have their own dock so they could go straight from their house out onto their boat.

In the past when there had been many fewer people on the island, houses had all been built facing the river. They had all had their own docks. So the preference to go straight from the house to the boat, while a luxury today, was in line with the old pattern.

For most of my growing up we did not have a boat. But my parents had friends who had boats and sometimes we would get invited out on their boats. This was understood to be a special treat, although sometimes these trips could be strange.

The Selbys had what to me looked like an enormous cruiser. Mr. Selby worked for AAA Insurance, but his heart was in his boat. And when they were not cleaning it or going out in it, they kept it docked and carefully covered up in front of their home on West River Road. My father once told my mother how much gasoline it took to take out and what it cost. She was appalled. My mother did not grow up with boats either. I remember one time we were invited out on the Selbys' boat.

Before we got aboard, we were all leashed up in life jackets. Then Mr. Selby cast off and we headed out into the river and downstream south toward Lake Erie. The boat had a smooth varnished finish all over that meant you could slip and fall easily. You had to hold on to stand up when it was moving. Mr. Selby was the captain and he carefully mapped out our way into Lake Erie. If there were other boats approaching we always passed on the right side. We waved to people on other boats, making sure to hold on carefully with our other hand. When we got to the end of the island, Lake Erie opened up and we saw how big it was. You could not see across it—it seemed endless.

There are five Great Lakes and Lake Erie is the second smallest. But that first time that I ventured out into it in the Selby's cruiser, I was truly impressed. What must the other lakes be like if this was one of the smallest? These remarkable fresh water lakes were formed at the end of the last glacial period as the glaciers receded. Mostly what I knew about the Great Lakes came from the book my mother read to us called

Paddle-to-the-Sea. It described the journey of a small wooden canoe with an Indian in it, carved by a young Indian north of Lake Superior, and set off through all five Great Lakes and out the St. Lawrence River to the sea. Along the way each Great Lake was described by its shape. Lake Superior, the largest, is like a wolf's head. Lake Michigan is like a squash with leaves. Lake Huron is like a trapper with furs on his back. Lake Erie is like a lump of coal. And Lake Ontario is like a carrot on its side. We also learned in school that the first letter of all the Great Lakes together spelled "homes." But I liked the shapes better, all except for Erie. Granted there were steel plants and coal yards along some of its cities, but a lump of coal was not distinctive to me and not good for a lake shape.

By the time I thought of all this, we were in the middle of Lake Erie. We could not see any land anywhere. So I went down inside the cruiser to feel safer. There was a kitchen, bedrooms, and a small bathroom they called a "head." I asked where we were going. Someone said, "To Put-in-Bay." I liked that name. It turned out to have been the place of a battle in the War of 1812, but they did not go into that for me in the middle of the lake. Later I learned that Commodore Perry had fought the British at Put-in-Bay in 1813.

In the first year of the War of 1812, the British had immediately taken over Lake Erie and recaptured Detroit from the Americans. There was a problem in that the British had ships in the area whereas the Americans' one ship was captured by the British. The Americans did not have other ships on Lake Erie to counter the British. They had to build them which they did in Erie, Ohio, on the southern shore of Lake

Erie. They also had to staff them and equip them with cannons and guns. At the same time the British were having supply problems of their own to the north at Fort Malden by Amherstburg.

Eventually the two forces set off against each other on September 13, 1813, by Put-in-Bay on South Bass island in Lake Erie, north of Ohio. The British under Commander Barclay had six vessels and the Americans under Commodore Perry had eight vessels. It was a difficult battle in which there were many fatalities and Perry's ship, the Lawrence, surrendered, but Perry went to another ship and was able to defeat Barclay from that ship. This American victory led to the recapture of Detroit and the eventual defeat in Ontario of the Indian leader Tecumseh who had been allied with the British.

I went to sleep on a bed in the Selby's cruiser and when I woke up we were at Put-in-Bay. There above the harbor was a tall statue of Commodore Perry for his victory against the British. Around the Bay the island had more docks and boat people than I had ever seen before. Boat people like to look at other people's boats and show off their own boats. They also like to sit on the backs of their boats, drink, and talk. It did not seem so exciting to my sister and me. Their excitement must be when they are out on the water, so dockside, they relax. I had slept through most of Lake Erie and wanted to explore the island, but we were told not go out of eyesight. Soon it was time to return.

Besides big cruisers like the Selby's, more common on Grosse Ile were smaller boats with outboard motors. Young men commonly had these. They would buzz around the island in them. In the summer, some people would water ski off the backs of them in the shipping channels. Some people even liked to try to get close to the freighters that glided by. Once my brother told me of an outboard motor boat that was playing tag with a freighter and got close, only to have a girl bounce overboard. Luckily, the driver was able to turn around quickly, someone grabbed onto the girl in the water as they sped a safe distance from the freighter, and they pulled her back in.

There were also people on the island who had sailboats. One of them was a friend of my father's, a Mr. Devlin. He had a Thistle, that is, a seventeen-foot sailboat. Mr. Devlin had grown up on the north shore of Lake Superior and therefore could not swim. The water had been too cold. He had come south to Detroit before heading off to Cornell College, but then the Depression hit and there was no money for college. He ended up working in a small parking lot in Detroit. He said he determined there had to be something interesting about parking lots. Eventually he became an expert on parking lots and designed them all over the world. Meanwhile in his spare time he sailed and talked to my father about the pleasures of sailing. He also gave my father a tip on some uranium stock in Canada. My father actually bought some of this stock and made money. Mr. Devlin convinced my father to buy a sailboat like his with the money.

My father however had never sailed before, nor had my mother. A Thistle has a main sheet and a jib, that is, a large sail and a smaller one. We would go out from the yacht club by Hickory Island into Lake Erie. My mother was a good sport but we could see it made her nervous. My father would be at the tiller, and my mother would have to move back and forth as they tacked or zigzagged into the wind, ducking to avoid being hit as the mainsail moved back and forth. My sister and I would crouch up in the front by the jib. Sailing takes practice and since Lake Erie is fairly shallow, storms come up fast. Once we got towed in by the Coast Guard.

Still sailing is a beautiful way to move on the water. We watched all the powerboats zoom past. They smelled of gasoline. We would just glide with the wind. But it was nerve-wracking too. You needed to know the weather, the shoreline, the currents, and how to tack when the wind changed. Even people who knew all these could still get into trouble.

My father's sailboat had been named *Sea Skimmer* since the previous owner lived by the sea. I heard it was bad luck to change the name of a boat, but that name just did not work in the Great Lakes. My father renamed his boat the *Matrix*. If you said it wrong it was "Ma-Trix." My mother was not amused. I think he named it that after drinking beer with some friends. And boats took a lot of work. My father kept the *Matrix* in our garage so there was no room for a car anymore. He had to sand it and then varnish it in the winter. He did not enjoy that. The garage was narrow and cold and dark. My mother was relieved when he finally sold it.

Our favorite boats however were the freighters. We loved to watch them in the different channels as they sailed upstream to get iron from the mines in the north and then bring it back to the steel mills down in Detroit or Cleveland, or bring coal or grain up to the mills and granaries in Detroit. You could always tell the difference between the Great Lakes freighters and ocean-going ships. The ocean-going ships were shorter. They had to be shorter because of the waves in the ocean. The *Paul R. Tregurtha*, one of the longest of the Great Lakes freighters at 1013 feet in length, would have broken apart with ocean waves.

But why then did we call freighters "boats" if they were longer than the ocean-going ships? We grew up calling them boats, and it was not just islanders, but all local people in the Detroit area did this. It turned out there was a historical reason. Earlier travel and transport on the river had been by canoes, then by schooners or sailing ships. Later in the nineteenth century steamboats came in and took over from the schooners. Since everyone called them "steamboats," even though they were quite large, people took to calling all local vessels on the river "boats." It dates from that time.

As the freighters sailed by, we could read their names from the island, our eyesight was that good. Their names would be on the side of the boat and on the back too. There would be flags as well. The flag of the home country was always on the back, while they often flew the flag of the country they were visiting as a sign of respect near the front. But what we especially liked was the sound of the horns as freighters signaled to each other. They had their own code. It was as if the river was speaking. It was especially moving at night or in a fog or storm.

I was so sad to learn, after I moved away from the island, that the freighters took more to using telephones over horns in the 1970s. What a loss. Only occasionally now will you hear the sound of a horn from a freighter on the Detroit River in the fog. It brings back so many memories.

Great Lakes freighter in Detroit River. Photo by F. Trix.

From the Naval Air Station to a New School: A Disrupted Year

How to make people feel special was not something that people thought about when I was growing up. It certainly did not occur to islanders. Still, when my class learned at the end of fifth grade that we would be spending the first half of sixth grade at the Naval Air Station on the island, we were sure that it would be a special time.

We were called "baby boomers." We did not understand what that meant. It sounded to me as if we should be making a loud noise. What it seemed to mean in terms of schooling was that they did not have room for us so we kept getting moved around.

We had our first school years in the new central elementary school building through fourth grade. The recess equipment behind this building was very fine. It was all metal with a long slide, tall swings, and my favorite, a sort of octopus that you would run around and around, and then swing out on until you got blisters on your hands. Fifth grade was in the old high school building with the fire chutes from the second floor.

At the start of fifth grade we did not know where we would be for sixth grade.

They were building two new elementary schools, one in the northern part of the island and one in the southern part, but they were not ready yet. What to do with us for the next year? I wonder who had the idea to send us to the Naval Air Station for sixth grade? Probably it was someone who was driving home from the construction site of the new school in the southern part of the island because that is where the Naval Base was.

The south end of the island is quite different from the north end that comes to a narrow point. In contrast the southern part is shaped more like a crab with two uneven legs that are islands in themselves. Between them there is a sort of bay and the low land in the middle is where they built the landing strips and the Naval Air Station. The land is so flat it is a good place for runways. It also must be easy to spot from the air.

In the 1920s some people from Detroit decided they wanted to learn to fly and even floated a tin hanger down the river from Detroit to the island. Eventually the Detroit Aircraft Corporation was established and a flight training school. But with the Depression, the Navy took over the land, the runways, and the hangers. In the 1930s it became a place for training naval reservists, albeit without pay. After Pearl Harbor in 1941 things heated up.

During World War II over 5,000 navy pilots trained at what became Grosse Ile Naval Air Station, along with over 1,000 British pilot trainees. Grosse Ile Naval Air Station had an indoor Olympic-size swimming pool with high walkways. The pilots could put on all their gear and then jump off from the high walkways into the pool. It was good practice in case they were shot down and landed in the water. Then they could practice again in Lake Erie just south of the island. There would be people nearby to help in case they got in trouble since it would be wise to work things out ahead of time before they ended up flying over the ocean. There were also small landing strips on farmland on the American mainland where they could land on their solo flights.

As for the island, this influx of new pilot blood was exciting. It led to marriages with men not from the island and not even from the Midwest. Of the ones I knew of, several were not successful. Indeed the men were handsome. But I think the islander women underestimated the cultural differences for the pilots were largely from the east coast of America; the men did not understand quiet islander values. Not that island men all made good husbands either. Still after the war there were more problems in marriage than there used to be. But in general, people from the island used to understand each other better. At least that is what people said.

Since we did not know where we were going for sixth grade until the very end of fifth grade, like most fifth graders, we did not think about it. Fifth grade is a special time and for girls is a golden time. We do not yet know that we are not supposed to be able to do many things. I remember explaining in Miss Ruska's fifth grade class how a car worked. I had read about it in the *Wonder Books*. It never occurred to me that as a girl I was not supposed to be interested in that or be able to explain it. No one commented on it which was just fine.

Valentine's Day in fifth grade was a time to make boxes

with hearts on them and give classmates valentines. We wanted to get as many as possible. But if we did not, I do not remember being upset. Life just went on.

We had a field trip to Greenfield Village in Dearborn, Michigan. Henry Ford had assembled there what he valued, like Thomas Edison's laboratory where he had invented the light bulb, and the chair that Abraham Lincoln was shot in. There was also a huge room full of trains and locomotives. Greenfield Village is very different now and better laid out. Much of the inside part is now called "The Henry Ford Museum of American Innovation." But when we went the inside part was a jumble of trains and locomotives. My great-grandfather had known Henry Ford. My grandfather told me that his father had said that when Henry Ford looked at an engine, he looked at it the way some people look at a work of art. I tried to imagine the locomotives as works of art, but it did not work for me.

The summer after fifth grade my sister and I went back to camp in Canada. Now we knew where we were going so it wasn't so frightening to get on the train in Windsor in the evening and go to Toronto and on to Canoe Lake. I was still not a good swimmer and I learned I was not good at horse riding either. Canoeing was still what I loved and we went on another canoe trip. The month passed even faster. In August I turned eleven. Sixth grade would be an adventure this year for sure.

Getting all the sixth graders to the Naval Air Station wrecked havoc with the school bus schedule on the island. Recess in the morning had to be lengthened to make sure we all got there before class began. We had recess on the parade ground in the middle of the

Naval Air Station, across from the Bachelors Officers Quarters. That was the year I got braces on my teeth. I remember feeling all the metal in my mouth with my tongue and looking over at the Officers Quarters. It was a strange place for school.

Our classrooms were upstairs in an old building with wooden stairs, wooden floors, and a raised platform for the teacher in front of the blackboard. It was only our sixth grade classes, no other students from other grades. It felt lonely. There was no gym. There was only a larger room where we met for some sort of indoor activity when it rained. Mostly we went outside on the parade ground for team sports. There were no field trips; we were living a field trip. Thankfully the fall passed quickly.

Meanwhile they were working to finish the new elementary schools. Our classmates reported on them regularly to us. Several of the boys had gotten in one of the new schools and said that the girls' bathrooms for the sixth grade had comb-machines. There was a strange silence. They were for sanitary napkins but no one could tell them that.

We were relieved when we left the Naval Air Station. We had been excited to go there because it had seemed so special. But in going to class there we had seen that it was old and not in good shape. We were there in 1959. Ten years later in 1969 when Secretary of Defense McNamara was closing bases around the country, he decided to close our base. He said it was too small to be made into a jet base, and the islanders certainly did not want jets.

Mrs. Jones, our sixth grade teacher, shepherded us to the new building. She was an experienced teacher and made what would have been a difficult year a relatively good one. I remember our international event when we dressed in different costumes of different countries. It was like a grown-up Halloween. I wore a Russian dress from Mrs. deBeausset's Russian mother-in-law and Suzanne wore an Indian sari. I found a Russian grammar book that my father had. He had wanted to study Russian history at one time but found the language too hard. From the grammar I came up with several lines in Russian that I recall to this day. We wrote out for Mrs. Jones what we wanted to do when we grew up. I wrote that I wanted to go to Middlebury College, known for foreign language study, and to be in the Foreign Service. I did go to Middlebury College but left after two years. It reminded me of summer camp, only that was not what I wanted in college. But I was not destined for the Foreign Service. Despite my language skills, I would never have been able to put up with the bureaucracy.

During sixth grade, one of the island churches offered seminars on sex education and our parents signed us up gratefully. The speaker was a woman who did not say anything memorable and the little booklets she gave out were worse. We were eleven- and twelve-year olds so we needed to know things if we didn't already. I do not recall being particularly interested, certainly not by this seminar.

The next year was junior high, what they now call middle school. We would be returning to the old high school, the one with fire chutes. At least that was familiar.

Frances in fifth grade after braids and before braces.

Sock Hops and Never a Cheerleader

Returning to schooling, it was a great relief to go back to the old high school for junior high where we had gone for fifth grade. But junior high was different enough in itself. For the first time we had different teachers for each subject and they were a mixture to be sure. My father had always said that putting up with bad teachers was part of life. Still, by and large they were fine.

For the first time I had male teachers as classroom teachers. Mr. Papp was our seventh grade science teacher. He taught us the scientific method, and smelled of the cigarettes he smoked. I liked his no nonsense way in the classroom. Mr. Goodhue taught geography and from him I learned about the fertile triangle in the Soviet Union. I knew very little about the Soviet Union and its size impressed me. It was 1960 and there were many new nations in Africa. We had to learn all their names and where they were. We took this personally—why so many and why this year? I loved maps so geography was something I cared about, but all those new African nations was a stretch. Mr. Tecmire, the

American history teacher, plodded slowly through the textbook. Partway through the term I remarked in class that if we did not go faster we would never get to the twentieth century wars. I had read my father's books on foreign wars and was interested in World War I and World War II. Mr. Tecmire took this personally and made me outline the chapter on Reconstruction after the Civil War. That was the year of the Kennedy-Nixon presidential race. One of the students in our class was even for Goldwater. She was repeating what her father said, one of the pilots from the east who had married an island girl. My brother later had Mr. Tecmire for ninth grade science, and for track.

There were women teachers too. Mrs. Bess, who was very nice, taught something called "General Languages." It was about languages, mostly European languages. But I wanted French and this was not French. We also had gym class with Mrs. Hottinger in the old gym where we had gone for the talk on shells many years before. We played girls' basketball that had antiquated rules such that you could not run the length of the court but had to stop halfway. It slowed down the game considerably. I do not know when they changed to rules to conform to how boys played but that was a distinct improvement.

We also had sock hops in that old gym. That is what they called our dances. We were deeply awkward. There were chairs along the walls. You could sit in the chairs or try to dance. I do not think islanders were great dancers. We did not get much experience. On television people had seen the program, "American Bandstand," where people could really dance. That was not us.

My grandmother paid for me to take ballroom dance classes at Arthur Murray off-island. She had met my grandfather at a dance after high school and felt all young women should know how to do ballroom dancing. I had liked dancing from my time with ballet. So once a week I went to Arthur Murray in Wyandotte and danced with a male teacher. He was a good dancer and I learned how to do the waltz, the rumba, the foxtrot, the cha cha, the tango, and something called the marengi. I liked the waltz and the Viennese waltz the best. I would come in from playing field hockey the last period of school, all sweaty and then get to dance across the expanse of the room with the young teacher in a waltz. I still had braces and a ponytail. It was an awkward time.

Still I remember what it felt like to sweep around the room. Needless to say, none of my classmates at Grosse Ile Junior High School did any of these dances. Swing might have been more useful.

The summer after seventh grade my sister and I again went to camp in Canada for the fourth time. Our canoe trips were getting longer. There was a cabin where all the girls had names that were forms of Elizabeth: Beth, Liz, Lizzie, Liza, Eliza, Bess and Betsy. After the queen of course. They had a dance too at Wapomeo with boys from the boys' camp Ahmek across the lake. It helped if you had an older brother whose friends might dance with you. I did not.

Back on the island we all passed into eighth grade which was held in the same old high school building. Again it was good it was familiar since we were changing. We were thirteen year olds, an age of change and maturing. The boys would sometimes run their hands down our backs to see if we had a bra on. I was not interested where their minds were. But we were not always a kind lot. I remember our eighth grade Sunday school class at St. James Church. There was a new teacher that year and he did not seem all that secure. We took advantage of that. In the second class we told him that none of us believed in God. That took him by surprise. He did not know what to say or do. He resigned. I do not remember what happened next. But it was not a kind thing to do.

We had a remarkable math teacher, Mrs. Sells. She would be with a group of us through most of high school for which we were most fortunate. She was highly intelligent and organized. She brokered no nonsense in her classes. I grew to look forward to math every day. She was part of special math group that came out of the Sputnik crisis—fear that since the Russians had beat us to put a vehicle in space, they were ahead of us in math and science education. It published an experimental math series known as SMSG—School Mathematics Study Group. Our class became part of this project. Anything Mrs. Sells presented we would have taken to.

Eighth grade was also the time for home economics for girls. I think the boys took shop. I was not a natural in home economics. In fall semester it was cooking and in winter semester it was sewing. I had no interest in either of these areas. I now wish I had paid more attention to my mother's cooking, but she shoed us out of the kitchen, saying anyone who can read can cook. That is patently untrue. I would have liked to have learned some of her dishes. But eighth grade was not where I was likely to learn much of any home craft. It was like phonics in first grade. I survived it.

I had done some early cooking at home in our kitchen. I had wanted to make a cake but was more interested in color than taste. When the batter was too light, I had added something to make it darker and then put it in the oven. It had exploded. I do not remember what I had put in. I remember too the first time I cracked an egg and what the shell felt like as my little fingers went into the yoke. Mostly we liked to lick bowls when my mother was making something good, like chocolate chip cookies. But my mother was an efficient cook, and we were outside most of the time. All of which is to say I was not prepared for cooking in home economics. It slid by me.

Sewing looked worse. I had started a knitting course at the Youth Center on the island one summer when I was seven. I knitted a long narrow piece in bright blue yarn that curled in on itself. My mother had asked me what it was. I told her it was a telephone cord cover. That was the end of my knitting. In sewing we were all supposed to follow a pattern and sew a dress that we were to wear in a fashion show at the end of the year. This would be quite a stretch for me.

I had gym class first period in eighth grade. That spring there were tryouts for cheerleaders. Most of the girls wanted to be cheerleaders. This was something I had never considered. To be a cheerleader you had to be able to do flips. I had never done a flip in my life. But I thought, at least I can try. So one morning in gym class I tried to do a forward flip. I landed wrong and came crashing down on with my right leg bent under me. Mrs. Hottinger, the gym teacher, tried to straighten out my leg. I shrieked. They called my mother and then helped me downstairs to get changed from my red gym suit into regular clothes. I was not in a good way. My mother took me to Dr. Bennett's office in Southgate where they took x-rays. My leg was broken.

This was the time when they put huge plaster casts on broken legs. Although the break was close to my ankle, Dr. Bennett put a cast on my right leg up to my hip. It was heavy and stayed on for three months. That was the end of cheerleading and gym class for me. It also made life difficult for me in the old high school building since there were many flights of stairs that I had to hop up and down. I had crutches that fit under my armpits and that hurt. I would finish my homework during gym period. I hated sitting in special chairs.

At home my mother was especially kind and thoughtful. I read a lot, books like Lady Murasaki's *Tales of Genji*, about eleventh-century Japanese aristocracy, books that only my mother knew about. Bathing was difficult and so was dressing. The cast was an ugly white that got uglier as the months passed. In my boredom, I cut out the dress I had chosen for home economics in one day at home. It was blue and white striped cotton with white zigzag material that I sewed on at the neck and waist. I sewed it equally fast at school. I had no patience. When the fashion show came, it was good that I was still in my cast and walked with the crutches under my arms. No one could see how poorly it fit. On the way home, we stopped at a dumpster and put the dress in. That was the end of it.

Finally it was time to get my cast off. I had been looking forward to that day. Three long months and finally it was cut off. My leg looked awful. It was thin and scaly. It did not look at all like my other leg. The doctor said it looked fine to him. He gave me no advice on how to get back walking. There was no rehab. I was expected to just start walking again. And so I did, slowly and awkwardly.

I remember trying to walk on Macomb Street with other students. I could not keep up.

This was familiar to me. Again, I could not walk right. I was thirteen and again I was not right in the way I walked. Some things never change.

PART THREE:

Island Life and Landmarks

Christmas on the Island: Falling off the Front Stoop

Holidays are probably the oldest social events on the island besides family gatherings. The holidays are associated with seasons, with Easter in spring and Christmas in winter. But spring in Michigan is not predictable. Sometimes it can even snow in April. Easter isn't predictable either as it moves around. I always associated Easter with the Easter eggs that we dyed each year, with the chocolate bunnies that we got in our Easter baskets, and with jelly beans. My mother would hide jelly beans all over the house so we could have jelly bean hunts. As for Christmas in winter, at least it comes on the same day each year. And winter itself is more dependable. It follows fall which is the most beautiful season on the island.

Fall starts with days slowly getting cooler. It feels good just to be alive and outside. The leaves on the trees slowly change as the maple trees turn crimson, and what is left of the elms turn yellow before they fall to the ground. After fall, winter comes quickly and it gets dark early. It was even still dark when we waited for the school bus at the corner of Colonial Court and Church Road every morning before school.

People looked forward to Christmas as the important time in this dark season. The island put on its finery at this time. Especially the houses along East River and West River Roads would be decked out with Christmas tree lights. It was as if the island was strung around with multi-colored lights. I wondered what it looked like from the river or even across from the Canadian shore. Could they see how lovely it was?

In my family in the middle of the island Christmas began much before the cold weather set in. My mother would begin playing records of Christmas carols in August. It is fair to say they were among her favorite music. And these were not popular renditions like "White Christmas," but rather classical and traditional carols from earlier times by famous chorales. So when people complained about having the J.L. Hudson Christmas parade in Detroit at Thanksgiving, that it was too early, we laughed. We had been celebrating Christmas at home for months.

One August my mother even got an early gift, an unexpected one. We heard a scream from my parents' bathroom and ran to see what had happened. There was my mother with a towel wrapped around her looking horrified down at the bathmat in front of the shower that she had just stepped out of. On the bathmat was a gift from our dog. A bloody chicken head! It was slaughter time for the chickens by Westcroft Gardens and our dog had chosen one head, brought it home, and carefully deposited it on the bathmat for my mother. It was a gift none of us forgot.

The fall passed and soon it was Advent. My mother found Advent calendars for us. You were only supposed to open one paper window each day all through the season of Advent. Patience has never been my strong suit and these calendars irritated me. I would try to hold them up to the light to see what tiny picture there was behind each closed window.

Christmas cards were a big part of Christmas for my mother. She wrote and sent many Christmas cards. She then kept the ones she received in a large glass bowl. People of her generation kept track of each other through this custom. It was a major undertaking. A few people would send form letters that told of all the activities of their family over the year. We saw that as a cop-out. These were instead of actually taking the time to write a personal note. My mother wrote personal notes to everyone.

Our house celebrated Christmas too with pine branches all over the house. We had wooden Christmas figures that marched across the mantel over the fireplace in the living room to a crèche. These figures included sheep, shepherds, the three wise men with their gifts, and of course Joseph, Mary, and baby Jesus in his cradle. One year the beloved dog of a neighbor on Church Road died. The neighbor brought us a small dog in his memory and we put that by the crèche too. All the time we had Christmas music playing.

Of course we had a Christmas tree. I loved the smell of the tree in the house. When I was four and my father was busy putting up Christmas tree lights on the tree, he told me not to put my finger in the socket of the lights. That had not occurred to me before. I looked at the socket. It was just the size of my finger. So I put my index finger in and got a shock.

Now I understood why he told me not to do it. That was when Christmas tree lights were like the bulbs of big flowers, not delicate the way they are today. We strung them from the top down. There was also a star on the top. When I was seven I remember stringing popcorn to put around the tree. Only I ate more than I strung and threw up all that night. I have never liked popcorn since then.

The weekend before Christmas, if you were good, you might get to drive around the island with Mom, delivering small gifts she had gotten for her women friends for the holiday. Another treat was to go around the island looking at the Christmas lights that people had put outside all around their houses. In the early evening when it was already dark, we would drive around the island to see the houses, all lit up for the holiday. We would do this several times during the Christmas season.

At church there was a lot of carol singing. My favorite was when they had a bass sing the haunting advent hymn alone, "O come, O come Emanuel" at the beginning of the service. I do not remember Christmas pageants. That took organization and that was not a strong point at St. James. We were better at just singing. I have no recollection of the theological meaning of Christmas. Perhaps we did not pay attention. I do remember when Mary Hascall, Mrs. Hascall's daughter, would say the line from the Twenty-Third Psalm, "Good Mrs. Murphy will follow me all the days of my life." It was years before I connected that with "Goodness and mercy will follow me all the days of my life."

In church we sang the usual Christmas carols. But from my mother's records, we learned other ones as well. One of my favorites was "The Cherry Tree." It felt right to me as an islander.

When Joseph was an old man, an old man was he,
He married virgin Mary, the queen of Galilee.
He married virgin Mary, the queen of Galilee.

Then Mary spoke to Joseph, so meek and so mild,
"Won't you gather me some cherries, for I am with child."
"Won't you gather me some cherries, for I am with child."

Now Joseph flew in anger, in anger flew he.
"Let the father of the baby gather cherries for thee."
"Let the father of the baby gather cherries for thee."

The cherry tree bowed low down, bowed low down to the ground.
And Mary gathered cherries while Joseph stood around.
And Mary gathered cherries while Joseph stood around.

Just before Christmas, in our neighborhood, a group of us young people would go out caroling in the evening from house to house. Tony Hascall had a good voice. He was a boy soprano and could hit the high notes of "Silent Night." The rest of us would sing along. We were good at "We Three Kings of Orient Are," and "It Came Upon a Midnight Clear" because the notes were not high. We would walk to a house, climb up on the front stoop, knock on the door, and start singing. We would do three carols. If it were really cold, and Michigan winters can be bitterly cold, some people might be kind enough to give us hot cider. Mostly though they just clapped and thanked us. Sometimes we got silly and people fell off the front stoop into the bushes or snow. The singing kept us warm.

None of us were interested in Santa Claus. It made no sense. We knew no person of his size could ever fit through our chimney. We had all climbed on the roof and knew how small the chimney was. And there was no need of an extra person to bring gifts. We all liked to wrap gifts and knew how long Mom had been working to get gifts for people.

On Christmas morning we were allowed to get up early and take our stockings into our bedrooms before breakfast. There would be gifts under the tree but those were for after breakfast. In our stockings would be books and maybe some trinkets. Mom was good at picking books that enthralled us. I later realized that my education came from my mother and the classic books she found for me. Finding a book in a Christmas stocking is special.

After breakfast we opened presents. We had to remember who had given them to us because thank you letters needed to be written within a few days. We cleaned up the boxes and gift paper. I wanted the Christmas tree to stay up as long as possible in the house, but the needles would start dropping off. Usually Twelfth Night was the longest it could stay up. They say that is when the three wise men came. I always thought they were late if that was so. We would then take the old Christmas tree to outside the Youth Center in the center of the island where other people brought their old Christmas trees. They would burn them there.

During Christmas vacation we always hoped for snow so we could go sledding or tobogganing down the Nixdorfs' hill into the canal that would be frozen over by then. On a toboggan there could be many people piled on top of each other. The more people, the faster it went down the hill.

What does all this have to do with the birth of Jesus in Bethlehem? It gave narrative to the Christmas carols and the characters of the crèche. But most of the festivities were more that of a mid-winter festival that you need if you live in a cold climate where it has been dark for a long time. People need to celebrate and sing to keep up their spirits. For some people that means eggnog, which I always thought disgusting. Hot cider is much better. And having many-colored lights all around an island in the middle of a dark river is also wise.

Gardens and My Mother's Fountain, the Porch Piano, and Appearances

In springtime when it finally came, many people worked in their gardens. Gardens were important to people who lived on the island. I came to see this as a difference between people who visited the island and islanders. People who visited the island and drove around the river roads, noticed the houses there, whereas islanders were more concerned with people's gardens.

Islanders knew there were big houses on the river roads, often thanks to inheritance, but the quality of a person's garden was more telling. It had to do with a person's own work and sense of taste. A widow could make a beautiful small garden that other people admired. Islanders liked to look at other people's gardens wherever they were, including on back roads. There was even a Garden Club of longstanding.

I remember when Mr. Nixdorf declared one Sunday, "Her hat is as overplanted as her garden." He was talking about a woman who lived on Thorofare Road. Indeed the woman wore fulsome hats to church. That was a time when women wore hats and gloves too. But

Mr. Nixdorf was jealous of her garden. He also lived on Thorofare and his back yard was a steep hill that went down to the canal, good for tobogganing, but not for making a garden. The woman's land, further south on Thorofare was flatter and much better for gardening.

But my family was not into gardening. My father had happily bought a house at the end of a dead-end road where no one could see the yard. Unlike men on Church Road who mowed their lawns to perfection that all could admire, my father shared a lawn-mower with Mamu, the next-door neighbor, and spent the least time possible mowing our side lawn, hidden by the crabapple and pine trees. As for the back yard, it was behind the house and most of it was pine needles. At some point, Daddy got a load of bricks from a former brothel in Detroit and extended the patio out to where the sandbox used to be. Then the field began. Little back lawn and no garden. The only exception was we did have rhododendrons that we bought from Westcroft Gardens in the front of our house under the kitchen window.

As for my mother, she said she had a black thumb. But later on she did have an idea for the back yard. She told my father she had always liked the sound of water so a small fountain on rocks with a pond would be nice. My father built a small fountain and pond under the pine trees near the field out of old rocks and pipes. It looked nice there in the shade, and the sound of the water on the rocks was peaceful that first day.

But the second late afternoon when my parents went out to enjoy the new fountain, what did they find but the pond full of the neighborhood dogs! There they all bunched together in the small pond, happily grinning and enjoying the cool water as it splashed on their furry backs. My mother said that was not exactly what she had in mind. My father just shook his head. Over time he let the structure slowly fall apart and that was the end of my mother's backyard fountain.

The largest houses on the island were along the river roads. When people from off-island saw these large houses from their cars, they often thought all the people on the island were wealthy. But there were inner roads when I was little that had houses that people said still did not have in-door plumbing. There was much greater variety of incomes. There were the old farmhouses and houses where families had lived for generations. There were cottages on Hickory Island that were for summer people. These got changed into year-round residences. There were also big houses that had belonged to people like the Olds of Oldsmobile. This got divided into five different residences.

Now there are even bigger houses along East River Road that I am told belong to Indian doctors. They are impressive in their size and their views of the river. The property taxes were always higher along East River Road. My parents' dream was always to live on the river. When they retired they finally sold their house on Colonial Court and bought a second floor condo near Macomb Street on East River Road. From the balcony they had a view of the river, but Stony Island obscured their view of the shipping channels and Canada across the way.

By that time the island had changed a lot. Many of my parents' friends had moved away to be with their children and grandchildren or they had died. There were new developments all across the island and many new homes had come in. The new homes and subdivisions looked more orderly than the old island I grew up on. Were the people different?

When I grew up on the island, I don't think appearances were that crucial. People tried to look nice, but there was only one hair salon on the island at Four Corners. We went there to have our hair cut. I remember getting upset when my ponytail was cut. I looked better with shorter hair, but it was a big change. I suppose some people went off-island to get their hair done. Mostly though people did their own hair care. Mrs. Anderson on Church Road even knew how to give brush cuts to boys and men. Later there was a time of big rollers because we all wanted to have long straight hair. People did not wear much make-up. To buy clothing, people went to Trenton or into Detroit. Some people made their own clothing.

When we were younger we watched the *Mickey Mouse Club* and liked different Mouseketeers. I remember Calvin Quant in our class knew how to tap dance and even danced for Milky the Clown in television. That was special.

But on the whole, life on the island was sufficient to us. We all knew each other and each year in school we saw each other again. There were no surprises. It was difficult as we got older. How could you date someone who was more like a brother whom you had known since kindergarten?

We did have good music on the island though. A center of this was the school where many students took band or singing. There was a popular singing teacher named Mrs. Jaroch. I was too young to remember her well. I just knew she had red hair and died of cancer.

We had a very fine music teacher in elementary school named Mr. McDonald. He was working on a doctorate in music at the University of Michigan and somehow ended up teaching music on Grosse Ile. I think he was originally from Scotland. He taught us music by Carl Orff and songs in many different languages. He stayed with us when he had trouble with his adviser at the University of Michigan and ended up teaching first grade at Grosse Ile too.

My sister played the trumpet and then changed to the French horn. She used to practice a lot. I think I know every piece of music ever written for the French horn from listening to her practice every day in her bedroom next to mine. She even went on in music to the University of Michigan. She used to put her clothes in her horn when she traveled, but then when young people asked to see her instrument, she didn't want to show it to them since she had her underwear in the bell.

We also had piano lessons. My mother had grown up in Detroit where music was especially important. Detroit had many German immigrants in the nineteenth century who came in mid-century due to famines and the failed revolutions of 1848, and later in the nineteenth century when they did not want to serve in Bismarck's armies. They brought their musical traditions with them. People always say that the Motown singers had learned to sing in their Black churches. But the music programs in the Detroit schools were also excellent and had influenced them as well.

Our problem was we had no piano to practice on. Then my mother heard of a piano that was on the porch of a family on West River Road. If we could come and take it, we could have it. My father got some of his friends, and for a case of beer, they got the piano to our laundry room. It was not an impressive piano and had suffered on the porch. But it was fine for my sister and me.

One day my mother came home from doing errands to find an older man tuning the piano. She was surprised since she had not asked for this. We kept our doors unlocked and the man had just walked in and started tuning the piano. He announced to my mother, "It's no Steinway." That was an understatement. It turned out, he had been invited to tune a Steinway piano for the older Stantons on West River Road and had gotten lost. My mother straightened him out on directions. She also thanked him for tuning the old porch piano.

The piano teacher we had was Mrs. Kinsman. She was the wife of Cyrus Kinsman, the man who took photographs of people on the island. They were an old island family. Their son was one of the early graduates of the island high school, but he had gone off to Australia. I wanted to ask why, but that was a question you could not ask. There was a photograph of him diving off a cliff in Australia. It was in their living room where Mrs. Kinsman gave piano lessons.

Mrs. Kinsman was very old when she taught us. Her fingers were the color of the old piano keys in their house. But what I liked more than the piano lessons was when she talked about how she had studied piano herself much earlier in Berlin. She told me she had even seen the Kaiser riding on a horse through a famous park there. That must have been decades ago, before the First World War.

Appearances on the island were deceiving. Who could have guessed that Mrs. Kinsman had studied piano in Berlin?

Bazaars & Rummage Sales, the Toll Bridge, Volunteers, and Politics

There were always bazaars at the church to raise funds. Women would make or bring food to sell and there would be a gathering and people would come and buy the different foods, including cakes, pies, and jams. There would also be several rummage sales a year. People would gather all the things they did not want anymore—old toys, equipment whose purpose they had long forgotten, and clothing that they no longer wanted. In a bigger town, such things might have gone to the Salvation Army, but there was no Salvation Army on the island. I liked to think of these items circulating around the island because somehow people bought them. The people who worked in these bazaars and rummage sales were all volunteer women from the church.

My favorite memory from one of these events relates to the Toll Bridge. We lived nearer the north end of the island so we used the Toll Bridge as our connection to the mainland. When I was little I was convinced a "troll" lived underneath the bridge. It took awhile before I got straight what "toll" meant. There was a small booth on the side in the middle of the bridge, and a man stood in the middle of the bridge there to collect little paper tolls, that people had bought earlier, from cars coming both ways.

One day my mother went to pick up pies from a bakery in Wyandotte and took me along. We were going to take them back to St. James Church on the island for the bazaar. Mom put all the pies carefully across the backseat of the car, and with me in the front seat we headed back to the island. She must have been thinking of other things because we hit the bend before the Toll Bridge too fast. As we came up on the bridge, she realized if she stopped to pay the toll in the middle of the bridge, all the pies would slide forward onto the floor of the backseat. My mother was too practical for this.

She told me to hold on. We shot across the bridge without paying the toll, faster than we had ever gone. The poor man who collected tolls just stared after us as we passed. All the pies got safely to the church.

I also remember when my father had to get out of the car to help open the bridge one winter afternoon because it would not open. Long Great Lakes freighters would come from the north carrying ore or coal for the McClouth Plant, just south of the Toll Bridge. The mid-section of the bridge would swing sideways to accommodate the freighter as small tugboats helped it through toward the steel plant.

But that cold winter day the controls had frozen. We were in our car on the mainland side of the bridge. We could all see the freighter slowing coming down and the bridge not opening. My father got out of the car and ran up on the bridge and up the stairs to the controls area above the toll booth to help. Thank goodness they got the bridge open before the freighter ran into the bridge. When those large Lake freighters move, they are hard to stop. Twice, in 1965 and in 1992, freighters did actually hit the bridge. But my favorite bridge memory was still the one with Mom and the pies.

The most important volunteer group on the island is the volunteer fire department. They were founded in 1942 under Chief Reaume with fifteen volunteers. Before this islanders had to wait for fire assistance from Trenton or Wyandotte, and it was often too late. Now there are thirty-three volunteers. The number of fire engines has increased and there are two ambulances to take people to hospitals. The headquarters is on Macomb Street in the middle of the island. When there was a fire in the Middle School in 1976, they asked for assistance from the nearby communities of Riverview, Trenton, and Gibralter in bringing up water from the river.

My mother volunteered as a reader for the blind. But this was off-island. She had a clear reading voice and was very good at this. This was before audible books. Later when I was at the university, I did this too for a blind doctoral student. I read newspaper articles for him in his field of research into a tape recorder. Years later when I was interviewed on NPR (National Public Radio), he called me to tell me he would know my voice anywhere.

Another volunteer activity was teaching Sunday school. My parents did this my senior year in high school. They did not try to teach us theology which was wise. Instead they took us on trips to visit other denominations and faiths around the city of Detroit.

What I remember most was our visit to Temple Beth El, the old Jewish synagogue on Woodward Avenue in downtown Detroit just before it moved out to the northern suburbs. We heard a most remarkable cantor there.

There were also political offices on the island that were elected but unpaid like the school board. With all the new schools that needed to be built, the school board made major decisions. My father got elected to the school board in the 1960s. We did not talk about this, but he had not graduated from high school. He had been sent out to school in Arizona from Detroit for health reasons, but there he had gotten another lung disease and had ended up in bed in Los Angeles for several years. There he had a tutor whom his mother hired, a man who had been doing research in the Vatican library, but had needed to sharpen his pencil. Instead he left his research and came all the way east to Los Angeles where he tutored my father. Daddy did go on for graduate degrees in chemistry. Perhaps because he did not graduate from high school he valued it more.

There was a township supervisor, but that was a regular position. I do not know much about political parties on the island. People said islanders, unlike my father, tended to be Republicans, while the surrounding downriver communities were mostly Democrats. These Republicans would have been Eisenhower Republicans when I was young. My earliest political memory is the slogan "I like Ike." That must have been from the 1956 presidential election.

Voting was very important in my family. I knew my father had worn a Roosevelt button to the Detroit

Club when he was a young man and his mother had to be taken out in hysterics. Clearly my father was a Democrat from a Republican family. When I was first allowed to vote, my father came and picked me up from the university so I could come home and vote at the youth center on the island. He drove two hours to make sure I could vote.

Politics in Michigan was not so party-divided at the state level. There were governors like Governor Milliken, a Republican, that people from different parties voted for. And some of the Democratic senators, like Senator Phil Hart, have also been universally admired. Hart Plaza in Detroit is named after Senator Hart, as is the Hart Senate Office Building in Washington, D.C. Some even called Senator Hart "the conscience of the Senate." He is buried on Mackinac Island.

Parents' Parties, Sewing, Poker, and Choir

Along with volunteer activities, social life on the island for adults was various. But as a child growing up, I only saw their social life from the edges of my parents' lives. What I remember of the parties that my mother gave were the small round rolls that she was famous for and the chance we had before we had to go to bed to snatch a few. And I remember a dessert that my mother made of thin chocolate cookies, lined up with whipped cream into a sort of snake that was cold and delicious. We could see it in the icebox before the party and hope that a little would be left the next day.

There were neighborhood gatherings that began around dinnertime. Adults would get together outside and have cocktails. These were when the weather was good and they could go on for a long time. We children were often fed early. We played outside and watched the adults talking and drinking. There was a lot of drinking then. They had hors d'oeuvres of cheese and crackers and nuts which they kept away from us. Sometimes we watched television or played board games if we snuck into a main house and no one saw us.

At one party at our house, my older sister and Tony Hascall dropped a firecracker down the chimney. I was outside in the yard when it all happened. My father came running out of the house. Apparently one of the guests, Mr. Devlin, had been sitting near the fireplace and could have been hurt. My sister and Tony ran off the roof, tripping on a wire as they leapt off. My father did not catch them, but he knew who had done it.

More nerve-wracking for my mother than the usual party was when my father brought foreign guests home from work for dinner. Mercifully this did not happen too often. One time my mother tried to make a "traditional American dinner" outside on the grill. Only it did not heat up enough and the meat did not cook. After that Daddy said no experiments on foreigners and Mom gave up on "traditional American meals" and cooked inside in the oven which was more dependable.

Women stayed home and took care of children and the home, and shopped and cooked. That was just what women did. Most families had at least three children so there was plenty of work. Adding parties to this was a significant addition of stress and expense I can now see. Where did women learn to cook special dishes for parties? I have no idea. There was no Julia Child or any television shows on cooking then. My mother had *The Joy of Cooking* cookbook by Irma Rambauer, a widow from St. Louis. Mom had never cooked until she married at age twenty-one. I don't even think she was very interested in food. At dinner, when we had dessert, she would finish the salad. But she must have quickly learned how to make meals and then to design food for parties too. She would go food shopping one morning a week since she had to go off-island to a grocery store in Wyandotte to do this. She had to be organized since she would get all the food for the whole week.

Most men did not help in the kitchen or with the housework at all. My father never learned to cook. I remember when he retired, he thought he would help with breakfast one morning. So he asked my mother the measurements for making oatmeal. She had made oatmeal for thirty years and had long ago stopped measuring. She could tell by just looking how much oatmeal and how much water to put in the saucepan. She said she didn't know the measurements. "Then how can you make reproducible oatmeal?" asked my father. We all laughed. Mom made the oatmeal as usual.

There were also social gatherings of adults that were separate by gender. My parents both had gatherings like this. With the women, the evening was known as "sewing." A large group of women would go over to the house of one of the women after dinner when the dishes had all been put away. They would bring a bag full of things that needed to be mended or darned, along with their sewing boxes. When they came over to our house, we liked to peek around the hall corner to see what they were doing.

The women would come in, give Mom their coats, sit down, and start talking. They would have their bags of mending with them. But sometimes I am not even sure they took anything out. The noise level grew to a steady hum. Now I realize that many must have been lonely all day, taking care of children and doing housework. This time to talk with other women about shared concerns was golden. People did not have cell phones. There was no internet. If they did not have good neighbors or friends they could talk to on the phone, women could be without adult conversation all day long. When their husbands came home in the evening, they were often tired and not up to talking even though their wives were hungry for adult attention.

Part way through the evening there would be some food, maybe cookies, something simple. And there would be something to drink. What mattered most though was the talk and the time to be with other adult women. People used to say that women gossiped a lot. Maybe some did. But I think now in retrospect they wanted to talk with other adults and especially with women who understood what their lives were like. Most assuredly other women understood their lives better than their husbands could.

There was a woman named Mrs. Pittman who was a professional seamstress. She lived on the southern end of the island where West River Road turned in. When she was much younger, she had gone out west and come back with a daughter and the name, "Mrs. Pittman." We never knew the story or anything about a Mr. Pittman. Nor would we ask. But since she was the sister of the island historian, Miss Isabella Swan, Mrs. Pittman already had island roots and status. Needless to say, Mrs. Pittman never went to "sewing." Rather, everyone went to Mrs. Pittman when they needed important alterations done on a garment. She was truly skilled.

Mrs. Pittman also knew everything that was happening on the island. My mother went to her, I think, just to listen to her. Like her sister, she was also a skilled duplicate bridge player. She was truly an island character. Her daughter became a respected librarian in the Trenton Library System.

As for male gatherings, my father met with other men on a regular basis to play poker. This was very different from the women's sewing. Before poker night, my father would set up the card tables and chairs in the living room. He would get out the cards and poker chips too. The men would come in and there would be some conversation, but nothing like sewing. We children did not find poker night half so interesting as sewing, although we wondered about the card game itself. There were not as many people for one thing. It was quieter. But the men seemed to be having a good time all the same. The men also stayed later. I think they were relaxing after long days at work.

There were some people who engaged in amateur theatricals on the island. This had started in the 1920s and they called themselves the "Islanders." I never saw any of their performances. They put on the plays in the old high school gymnasium on the stage where the man who talked about shells and reefs had spoken. When I was in high school, my parents used to get together with friends to read plays aloud in private homes. Different people would take parts. I had taken typing one summer and for practice, I typed out seven versions of a famous play, one for each character. This was before copy machines.

An early form of socializing for adults was to serve in the choir at St. James Church. There was a choir director who led weekly practices every Thursday evening and singing in church on Sunday, along with holiday events. Every June the choir would go up north for a special weekend at the resort of Oscoda on Lake Huron. Some talk of what went on during this June weekend was problematic and the practice was eventually discontinued. When more churches came to the island in the 1960s, several people left St. James Choir. The choir weakened, but in the long run, it was better for the church.

Change, Churches, and "Look at the Natives"

People didn't like to think that things changed on the island. We had the same holidays. And for almost a hundred years we had largely the same two churches, one Protestant and one Roman Catholic. But things on the island did change, whether people were aware of it or not. In America in the early 1960s there was much change, although probably things changed more slowly on the island. I remember hearing that someone at an Island Parent Teacher Association meeting made the remark, "What is all this talk about busing? We have always had busing on the island."

As for change on the island, mostly what I recall were when new areas were developed for housing. I remember when what we used to call "Bambi's field," a large area of fields off of Church Road, was turned into a residential area. Then the area on the other side of Church Road, a much larger area, became what was known as "Potawatomi Woods," where many new homes were built. This is where they named a street after H.C.L. Jackson, the *Detroit News* columnist who used to live at the corner near where I lived and who had interviewed me and my sister when were little. Many people moved into these new homes and had children who went to island schools. Some were people whose fathers had relocated to the Detroit area for business reasons, but most were from Detroit or suburbs closer to Detroit who were moving away from the city.

Even Macomb Street changed some. There were real estate agents who opened offices there. Mrs. Saunders, who lived on the island, opened a small store for girls' clothing on Macomb. One of the ways she got customers was by holding a fashion show at St. James Church, the only place with enough room to have people gather and walk through. Young girls who frequented the store were asked to be models. Since many young girls had illusions of becoming models, this was quite a compliment. I was asked to model a lavender skirt and blouse outfit, and a swimsuit and towel combination. I was tall and thin which was why I was asked to model the swimsuit. I recall standing up on a platform in the black swimsuit in front of many mothers and other young women, and realizing I did not like it at all. So I held the big towel in front of me. Then I walked through the church hallway, past where I usually had Sunday school, towel in hand. It cured me of ever wanting to model anything ever again. I did end up getting my mother to buy the lavender skirt and blouse outfit however.

Even the churches on the island were changing. The religious history of the island had been spotty. Early on a French priest had wanted to set up a mission to the Huron Indians on Grosse Ile, but the Hurons had preferred to have it on the island of Bois Blanc (later known as Bob-lo) in 1742. Visiting Moravian missionaries on the other side of the river held services in German and in English for island tenant farmers in 1791 and concluded that the inland people "longed as little for the Word of God as the heathen did." The first documented religious service on the island itself was a simple Quaker one in 1793, but it was followed the next evening by the same Indians and white men who had been at the meeting dancing in a circle around a fire, hollering, and drinking in a way that that did not comport with the earlier Quaker meeting.

Catholic and Protestant visiting clergy came to the island periodically when they could get there. In the 1840s there were even five clergy living on the island but no churches. In the mid-1800s at one time there were ecumenical Sunday school classes for Catholic and Protestant children together. The Protestants and Catholics on the island had joint church socials and the menu was set: ham and chicken salad, campfire coffee, and homemade ice cream and cake. Three churches were finally built on the island around the time of the Civil War. St. John's Episcopal Church was organized in 1850 for Protestants northwest of the canal that ran through the island. It had a building on the corner of Church Road and West River Road, but in the twentieth century it would gradually fade away. St. James Episcopal Church, for Protestants on all other parts of the island, was opened in 1868 on East River Road and was long-lasting. In 1871 St. Anne's Church was founded for the Roman Catholics and it too endured, later becoming Sacred Heart.

Original St. James Episcopal Church (1868), now St. James Chapel.
Photo by F. Trix.

The funding for St. James Episcopal Church initially came from the life savings of a former slave, Lisette Denison, who worked for the Biddle family and other prominent Detroit families. She was illiterate but had invested in steamship and bank stock on tips from householders in families she worked for. In her will, she had left the larger portion of her savings for the funding of a Protestant church that poor people could attend, but did not specify where. Her executor, William Biddle, decided it should go to help fund a church on the island. I would have thought the funds should have gone for a church in Detroit. The Biddles then matched the amount she gave and so St. James was founded.

There is a special red door on St. James, thanking Lisette Denison for her gift. As a child, I had liked the red door. I also liked the large stained glass window above the altar of the church that is now the chapel. It is a Tiffany window and was donated by the Biddle family. What stood out to me as a child was that the central figure in the window, an angel, has dirty feet. It always made me feel more at home in church. But what Lisette Denison's gift says to me is that people from Grosse Ile now have a responsibility to give to the people of Detroit, since her gift should have gone there.

Lisette Denison Doors on St. James Chapel. Photo by F. Trix.

St. Anne's Catholic Church (established 1871), now St. Anne's Chapel.
Photo by F. Trix.

In the 1960s, other Protestant churches opened on the island—a Presbyterian church, and then a Baptist church, and a Lutheran church. This was real change. For the first time St. James had competition for Protestant parishioners. Before, people like my family, who had not been Episcopalians, had no choice but to join St. James as the only Protestant church on the island. In fact, my mother's parents had been Plymouth Brethren and my father's grandmother had been Swedenborgian—a somewhat unusual

Protestant faith. Johnny Chapman, also known as Johnny Appleseed, and the poet Robert Frost were also Swedenborgian.

To make matters more complicated, at the same time that the new Presbyterian church opened on the island, there was a split at St. James with some people siding against the main priest, a Mr. Hackwell, and others with a new assistant priest from South Africa, a Mr. Kay. Thus the 1960s were problematic in the oldest church on the island. The Episcopal bishop's response was to have all clergy resign from the parish, move elsewhere, and bring in a senior priest, a Father Herring from Ohio, who calmed the waters. Lloyd Hackwell left and went to Vermont. There was an assistant priest, Bob Shanks, who had worked with young people, who also had to leave. The priest from South Africa, Andrew Kay, went to Mariners Church in Detroit.

My father had been greatly impressed by Andrew Kay, so much so that he was even confirmed, something that he had resisted until then. Daddy used to go to church with us, but he dozed during the sermon that he found tedious. My mother coped with this by saying that the liturgy was so beautiful that we did not expect much from the sermons. That is until Mr. Kay came. Unfortunately Mr. Kay then died an early death at age forty. He had suffered terrible injuries from World War II on the beaches of Anzio in Italy, and these war injuries finally got the better of him.

The minister at the new Presbyterian Church, Richard Milford, turned out to be very popular on the island. He had planned to go to India one summer, but instead found that he needed to go to the South for

Civil Rights work. We had people who went south from Detroit, like Viola Liuzzo, a white woman from Detroit who drove south to Alabama and was killed there in 1963 as she was driving Black Civil Rights workers. My mother had me watch Dr. Martin Luther King Jr. on television that August when he gave the "I Have a Dream" speech from Washington D.C., something I have never forgotten. My mother had grown up with Black people on the east side of Detroit and knew how important this was. Not everyone on the island related to Black people and the importance of Civil Rights the way my mother did. Earlier I remember the first time I saw an Afro hairdo on the cover of the Saturday section of *The Detroit Free Press*. Things were changing in the Black community in Detroit but Grosse Ile was distant from this.

After the riot or rebellion in Detroit in 1967, my mother responded by driving for Focus Hope, a Catholic charity in Detroit. She would pick up Black mothers from their homes in Detroit and take them to the Focus Hope Center to get food for their children up to age five. I do not know anyone else on the island who did this at this time.

Rather, the country clubs on the island flourished. Earlier there had been golf courses on the island, but they were mostly for the people who just came for the summer to the island from Detroit; I cannot imagine many of the local farmers playing golf. We did not belong to any of them but liked to use their hills for sledding in winter. As more people came to the island, these clubs acquired more members.

While there was change on the island in the early 1960s, still there was much that had not changed. People tended to stay on the island. Families that had come in the first half of the 1800s, families like the Ruckers, the Lowries, the Reaumes, the Bouchers, and the Forshees had remained, and my classmates in school had the same last names as these early families. There were other families I knew whose ancestors had come from the middle 1800s, people like the Stantons, the Grohs, the Foxes, the Leuchtmans, and the Wilcoxes. Was there an island mentality?

One Sunday afternoon I was sitting with friends from the neighborhood on an old stonewall on the west side of the island by an old Mather property, just looking out across West River Road to the river. On Sunday afternoons people from off-island used to come and drive around the island on the roads by the river, around East River Road and West River Road. They would drive slowly so they could see the big houses by the river and see the river views as well.

One car passed us slowly as we were sitting on the stonewall and swinging our legs, and someone in the car said loudly, "Look at the natives!" We looked at each other in astonishment. "Who are they talking about? Natives?" But then it hit us. They were talking about us! Were we different? It had never occurred to us before.

Wild Swans, Long Windows, and Writing from a Grosse Ile Kitchen

A Detroiter, who had spent his summers on the island the last decade of the nineteenth century, returned to live there from the 1930s to 1961. He lived with his family in an old house on East River Road. He described the coming of the wild swans in the night as they paused on their migration north. In the morning there would be thousands of swans along the island shore, fluttering and swooping in flocks. There would be migrating wild ducks with them that fed on the weeds that the swans dug up. The birds with their long white wings stayed for about a week and then one morning they would be gone. The wild swans came in mid-April and were a sign of spring for islanders.

Only I never saw the wild swans. Pheasants were the only large birds I ever saw on the island. Granted I did not live by the river, but I went to church near there and would have seen them. Were they gone by the time I was on the island in the 1950s? Had they changed their migration routes?

The man who described the coming of the wild swans as a sign of spring, Sid Corbett, was the age of my grandfather. And like my grandfather, he grew up in Detroit. As a young boy, he used to come to the island in the summer, but he did not arrive in early spring or notice wild birds then. Like my grandfather, he went to France for the US Army in World War I. He returned and eventually ended up in the automobile industry. In his case he eventually became national truck sales manager for General Motors' Chevrolet. He was a big man and most active, traveling a lot for his work, and he courted Lucy, the woman who would become his wife, who was also from Detroit. Suddenly his life changed. He spent five years in the hospital. After that he and Lucy moved to the old Lowrie home on the island. What had happened?

At the height of his business prowess and at about the same age as Franklin Roosevelt, he was struck with polio and became paralyzed. In the hospital he began to write and wrote several children's books based on his earlier sailing on the Great Lakes. When he moved to Grosse Ile it was in a wheelchair that he would never leave.

From the long French windows of his room and the porch of the house on East River Road, he observed life on the river and the freighters as they passed. His wife Lucy, who had studied at the Sorbonne in Paris and was fluent in French, was a wonderful cook. Sid was gregarious and would sit in his wheelchair in the large kitchen where visitors came and sat and talked. People often came and stayed for meals, so Sid knew many islanders and listened to their stories.

I remember the Corbetts' house because my mother was friends with Katy, the Corbetts' grown daughter, who worked as a teacher in Riverview and lived with her parents and her two children. As you came up the long driveway from East River Road, there were smoke bushes on either side. You were greeted by several dogs, and a cat named Daniel Boone, pronounced "bone." The house itself was from just after the War of 1812. It was two-story and impressive with a wide porch on the front. It had been built by a Britisher who had been stationed at Fort Malden north of Amherstburg during that war who had liked the hunting and fishing across in Grosse Ile. He came back after the war with special materials, including a spiral staircase for the house on the island which he subsequently built.

There is a double front room with fireplaces at both ends. In the nineteenth century there used to be dances there with musicians, since it was one of the largest places on the island. They even had a French dancing master who would come from Detroit and teach people the dances. Sid used the left front room as his bedroom and closed the sliding door. The other front room was the living room that Lucy used for her gatherings, sometimes the Friday musicale.

Behind this was the spiral staircase. Upstairs I would play with Katy's daughter Anne. They had a large dollhouse peopled by the "illegitimate Plantagenets." We would go downstairs for lunch. They would give us peanut butter and bacon sandwiches on toast. The first time I thought what an awful combination until I tasted it. It was delicious.

The kitchen was huge. It had been added on later. There were three stoves: one gas, one electric, and one wood burning. Lucy would cook her wonders here and Sid would help by cutting up vegetables and meat.

I saw Sid in his wheelchair. He was a big man. I never met Lucy because she died in 1955, but I thought I knew her because I heard so much about her, and later read the two books that Lucy and Sid Corbett wrote about their life in the old house with the long windows, their many animals, and the meals they made in that large kitchen. The books were called *Pot Shots from a Grosse Ile Kitchen*, and *Long Windows: More Pot Shots from a Grosse Ile Kitchen.* They were compilations from their weekly "Pot Shot" columns.

What had happened was that while sitting in his wheelchair, Sid had started writing about their life in the old Grosse Ile house, what Lucy cooked and how she made it. It was cooking set in a home and the cultural context of the island and Detroit River, and so well and clearly written that it made you want to try the recipes yourself. These became a Sunday feature column in the Women's Section of the *Detroit News.* H.C.L. Jackson, the regular *Detroit News* columnist had encouraged Lucy and Sid. He wrote the preface to their first book of compilations.

Old islanders would visit and would often bring fish they knew how to find that had just migrated up Lake Erie. There would follow a recipe for fish and chips with the freshly caught pickerel and the fish eggs saved for breakfast. Lucy liked cold slaw with fish and chips so there was a recipe for this too.

In the fall islanders might bring them ducks and Sid would talk about earlier times going duck hunting around the marshes at the mouth of Lake Erie and how there were two kinds of ducks. There were the wild northern ducks, the canvasbacks and redheads, that migrated south in the late autumn and early winter.

These were becoming more rare. Then there were the local ducks, the teal, the mallard, and the bluebill. He would follow with a recipe for cooking duck, not an insignificant task, and the special sauce that Lucy made. After this he would describe a hunting escapade from an earlier time with duck decoys and sneak boats. He would close with a comment about not overcooking duck and the differences between wild and local ducks.

Some of my favorite descriptions are of soups that Lucy made. French onion soup is described in such a way that you want to make it right away. Even pea soup sounded enticing. There are spring soups like leek and potato, or a vegetable soup that islanders call "All That's Left," and a Bretonne bean soup. All are surrounded by stories of local people and lore. The story of Monique Navarre Macomb and her journey with her three-week-old son was within the "Pot Shot" of a recipe on baked beans and brown bread. Lucy had forgotten to get enough black molasses and someone had taken Sid in the car. So Lucy had to walk all the way to a store on Macomb Street to get the black molasses. On the way she thought of Monique Navarre walking all the way to Detroit and how her own walk was nothing in comparison.

Sid was most observant of life around their home, and of how food was cooked and meals put together. He also had an earlier view of the island and a man's view, both of which are different from my own. He was a remarkable writer—clear and memorable. I think of him writing from his wheelchair on a manual typewriter with respect. At the same time writing the weekly column probably helped save his soul. He had something he had to accomplish each week.

Lucy helped in the writing some too. At the end of their first book, there are "Pot Shots" that show how they worked together and wrote.

Sid tells of going duck hunting one Thanksgiving with his father who was a big duck hunter. He was only nine years old and this was up in the duck marshes of Lake St. Clair with a master hunter, a local Frenchman who had a restaurant up there. They went by train and launch, arriving in the dark the night before. It was early winter and bitterly cold. Sid described setting out early the following morning with two boats; the second boat had fifty wooden decoys, and some live decoys that were legal then, and an Indian. After paddling for an hour they set up the decoys and a blind, and waited for an hour. Nothing happened. Then some wild ducks flew over and the live decoys called out so the ducks turned in.

There was shooting and young Sid ended up in the bottom of the boat surrounded by dead ducks. It began to snow. He was freezing cold. Finally his father recognized how cold his son was and they went back to the restaurant where the wife of the owner had a tub of hot water ready for him. His father peeled off his clothes and plopped him in. The wife then gave him a special drink in a mug that made him sweat and warmed him through and through. He had no idea what was in that drink. Years later he described this to Lucy and she said she had been given this drink in a cold winter in Paris between the wars. She told him it what was in it and how it was made.

Thanks to Lucy, Sid then explained how to make this special French cocoa laced with brandy. Back to the small restaurant on Lake St. Clair, after warming up, they all ate duck for dinner. But what stayed in Sid's mind was the drink the wife had given him.

The last "Pot Shot" in that book is by Lucy. She links it to Sid's tale of his Thanksgiving in the duck marsh restaurant of the French couple saying that theirs was a French kitchen like so many others from Lake St. Clair down the Detroit River to Lake Erie as the last vestiges of old French Detroit. For according to Lucy, Detroit was French. She recalls the old stockade of Fort Pontchatrain that became Detroit. And for the French, the important holiday was not Christmas but New Year's Day.

It was *le Jour de l'An* when children would put their wooden shoes by the chimney to wait for Saint Nicholas. The mother of the house would prepare the table with all sorts of good food for the visit of the priest, who would visit the houses of his parishioners that day. There would be wine, venison, quail, ham, and brioches, with the place of honor for the special dessert.

The oldest person in the house would be given special respect that day, even by the priest when he visited. And all the women would be kissed by the men that day. When the priest came, he would be given perhaps some cognac along with the food. While he was there, someone would put presents in his sleigh outside as his yearly gift.

But the special dessert that sat in the place of honor on the table was *crème renenversée,* a sort of custard with a caramel topping. Lucy then proceeded to give the directions on how to make this "the queen of custards" of French Detroit.

In another source, not as a part of the "Pot Shot," there are accounts that on the island, New Year's Day was always a day that islanders kept for open house and all served refreshments. This may be left over from the old French custom.

Nineteenth-Century Fun, Girl Scouts, the Youth Center, and Lack of Crime

In earlier times on the island in the nineteenth century, the outdoors seems to be have been the setting for social events. In the winter there were skating parties on the East River, including even a masquerade skating party, along with sleigh and coasting parties. In the summer there were picnics and boating gatherings, with dancing outside on the pavilion at Sugar Island when it was open. There was even a two-week summer camping trip in the 1880s on Hickory Island with people from Detroit and Ann Arbor also invited. There were forty young people, all over the age of sixteen; that was truly memorable. This went on for six seasons. And for years afterwards, people would gather to remember these two-week camping trips.

In contrast I recall one of the earliest birthday parties I went to in the basement of a house. It was for the four-year-old daughter of one of my father's colleagues whose wife had died. It was a big party with lots of cake and ice cream and balloons. There was a photographer so we all were sent pictures of ourselves sitting in a basement looking confused with all the cake and ornaments around.

My mother did not make birthday parties for us children, other than family gatherings. My birthday was in August which was not a good time for parties since people tended to be away at this time. But once when I was little she did have a birthday party for me. She invited other little girls and a few of their mothers and we all went to the Belle Isle Petting Zoo in Detroit. Like the earlier events on the island it was outside. It was a great success. We loved seeing the animals and getting close to them. Many people on the island did not know Detroit the way my mother did and she was able to convince them to come and we did have a good time.

There was also scouting on the island. I did not know much about Boy Scouts. But I was a Brownie and then a Girl Scout. The uniforms were a pain to get ready and wear to school on the day of the meetings. And some mothers would have to agree to be leaders, what seemed to me largely a thankless task.

When my sister and I were little, my mother was a Girl Scout leader with Dr. Joanne Stryker. The Girl Scouts met at the Catholic school since it was a central location and near Dr. Stryker's house. We thought of the Girl Scouts then as "the green giants." They seemed so big to us. And how did a medical doctor like Dr. Stryker have time to lead a Girl Scout troop after work? Dr. Stryker was a gynecologist at the Wayne State University Medical School in Detroit, had done some of the basic research on birth control, and had much energy. I think my mother also had a high energy level. My sister and I were so little at this time that what I also remember about the Girl Scouts in the early 1950s is that they wore bobby socks.

By the time I was old enough to be a Girl Scout myself, my mother and Dr. Stryker were no longer leaders. Instead we had several other mothers as leaders. We would meet and sing songs together. We sold Girl Scout cookies every year to make money for the troop. I was not good at selling Girl Scout cookies because I could not sell cookies I did not like and I only liked the mint cookies. I sold two boxes to our neighbor, Mrs. Kronk. But I told her not to buy the peanut butter cookies. The husband of our leader worked for Ford Motor Company and was high up in design. He took the Girl Scout cookies to work and sold many boxes. We thought that was cheating, but probably we were jealous since we knew our fathers would never take Girl Scout cookies to work to sell.

We were supposed to be working on merit badges. They looked good on the sashes of our uniforms. But our leaders were not especially gifted in the different areas. Still they gave of their time. I remember a camping trip that we had on the southern part of Grosse Ile. We put up tents, but the leaders worried that it would rain. We ended up staying inside someone's house. No one was really into camping in our Girl Scout troop on the island. This must have been different from those who stayed for two weeks on Hickory Island in the 1880s.

Our main leader was a Christian Scientist. That is the American religion founded by Mary Baker Eddy around 1875. This did not have anything to do with Girl Scouts. But she told our family about the newspaper, *The Christian Science Monitor*. Our family started getting the newspaper that came five days a week from Boston. The *Monitor* had a broader notion of the news that included positive events, as well as international news that our *Detroit Free Press* did not cover. I got used to reading the *Monitor*. When I went away to college, I got a subscription to the *Monitor* so I would always have something in my mailbox, five days a week. Later I kept up the subscription. I am sure that I was educated in international news by the *Monitor.* I always thanked the Girls Scouts for this.

Grosse Ile also had an old barn in the middle of the island on Meridian Road called "the Youth Center." During the summer, craft classes were offered there. I had taken a course in knitting there when I was seven. During the school year, on Friday evenings there were gatherings for high school students after the football games. People would get together downstairs and talk. Then they could go upstairs where it was dark and there was recorded music playing and people could dance. There would be two adults who were supposed to be supervising. They would go upstairs periodically to see how people were behaving. It could be deeply awkward.

There was also a wildlife sanctuary on the island by the canal and Thorofare. So much of the island itself was like a wildlife sanctuary, we sometimes wondered why they needed a special one. Now that the island is more developed it makes more sense. But when we were growing up, we could not figure it out. Some people said it was a good place to go to make out.

There were two police cars on the island. By the second week of school, we all knew the unmarked car. The police did not like to pick up island kids. They were more interested in dealing with off-island people. I do not remember any crime—there was no need—although I know drinking could be a problem. Sometimes speeding was a problem too. I remember when a popular girl was going so fast on West River Road that the car she was driving careened off the road and sailed way out onto the water. It was good she was going so fast or she might have landed in the shallows which would have been more dangerous. Thank goodness she was all right.

A high school student once was speeding along Church Road, and when he hit the bridge over the canal he killed our dog. But no one would ever have called the police. My brother remembers a friend of his climbing up on top of the Free Bridge. Not a wise thing to do. But the police were not involved. Young people did dumb things, but the police were themselves islanders and they understood.

Recently I have seen Grosse Ile Township declared the safest place in all Michigan. That is because it had no violent crime and only twenty-nine property crimes in one year. In general, the Downriver area is safe with Trenton rated high for safety on the list as well. With Grosse Ile, I imagine people with ill intent would have to know the geography of the island which can be confusing. Also the bridges make it easy to trap someone. And it is not close to getaway highways.

When I grew up on the island, we did not lock our doors at night. I went off to college and unwisely I left my bicycle out, unlocked, the day I moved in. It was stolen that first day. My mother, who grew up in Detroit, always locked the doors of the car in the city.

"Do not tempt people," she would say, as she put any packages in the trunk. But on the island, we knew what other people had. We might covet it, but in general we would not take it. It was theirs. Perhaps that is a sort of island mentality, which, with the geography of the island, mediated against crime.

Landmarks of the Island: the Lighthouse, the Pagoda, and the Wonder Well

The most obvious landmarks of the island were the two bridges, the Toll Bridge that was built in 1913, and the Free Bridge that was built in the 1930s. But these were fairly recent. Westcroft Gardens on the west side of the island also became a landmark in the twentieth century with its walking paths and greenhouses. It had been a simple hay farm in the same family for many generations until Ernest Stanton turned it into commercial gardens in the 1920s. Another obvious landmark was the Naval Air Station on the south end of the island. When the Grosse Ile Naval Air Station was closed in 1969, the question was what to do with the hangars? The airfield stayed and some private planes used it. But the hangars were so large. At first some were turned into tennis courts and others were used partially for making dried flower bouquets. Now the township offices are in Hangar One, and the Grosse Ile Historical Society has a museum there.

The oldest landmark of the island is the canal that winds through the northern half of the island on a diagonal and comes out by the Free Bridge. Several roads have bridges that cross the canal. These include Parke Lane, Horsemill, Church Road, Ferry Road, and Meridian. As we learned to drive, going over these bridges could cause problems.

Another landmark was the Grosse Ile Lighthouse, or should this be called a "river mark?" You cannot see it from the road because it is in front of a house that is private property on the northeast side of the island. But it is clear enough from the water. There used to be two lighthouses, both at the north end of the island and both from the 1890s, but there is only one left. It is in front of the Devlins' house and since my parents were their friends, we often went there and walked out to the lighthouse.

It is not a large lighthouse, and in the 1960s it was decommissioned. But the Grosse Ile Historical Society worked to preserve it and even to make sure it was kept in good condition. There is something reassuring

The Grosse Ile North Channel Front Lighthouse. Photo by James Marvin Phelps/flickr.

The Pagoda, formerly owned by Harry Bennett. Photo by F. Trix.

about a lighthouse. It signals to boats that here is land, and to land that there are boats traveling nearby. The presence of a lighthouse makes people feel that they are being taken care of. Perhaps we have sea-going genes in us that recall the fear of reefs or of crashing on rocky shores. A light guiding the way does reassure us.

Yet another island landmark is the Pagoda. This is an unusual boathouse on West River Road on the northern part of the island. It is truly distinctive due to its handsome Chinese architecture. Henry Ford had bought land from West River Road to Meridian with the intent to build a house there in the 1920s. But allegedly Mrs. Ford worried about the currents in the Detroit River and thought they would be dangerous for the children, so nothing was done with the property. In the late 1930s Ford had his henchman, Harry Bennett, supervise construction and the boathouse was finished in 1939. Ford sold it to Harry Bennett.

Henry Ford had hired Harry Bennett as head of his Internal Service Department to control labor unrest and suppress labor unions in the 1920s, 1930s, and 1940s. Bennett was a former boxer and sailor, and used intimidation and violence in the plants. He had many enemies and so he was careful about his own security. It is said that each room in the Pagoda has at least two exits, although one might be hidden. Besides the obvious way out to a boat from below the house, there is also a tunnel from the Pagoda under the road to a small building on the other side of the road, so you could leave from a vehicle kept there as well. When Henry Ford II took over the Ford Motor Company in 1945 from his grandfather, he finally fired Harry Bennett.

Sadly, the Pagoda's beauty was greatly diminished by the building of a large steel plant, McClouth Steel, just across the river from it on the mainland. This was finished in 1954 and made that whole northwestern shore area of Grosse Ile less attractive. McClouth Steel would spew out clouds of soot and noise, and since winds were from the west, the pollution all came to the island. By the same token it provided many jobs for people in downriver communities.

McClouth Steel became the ninth largest steel producer in the country. It was the first to use computers on a hot strip mill in the early 1960s. It had multiple blast furnaces and used a continuous casting process. At one point there was talk of Great Lakes Steel, an even larger steel company in Ecorse and River Rouge, merging with McClouth. But Great Lakes was owned by a man named Campbell. And Mr. McClouth was known to have said, true to his Scots background, "You canna trust a Campbell." There was no merger.

McClouth Steel was sold in 1996, and eventually closed in the early 2000s when cheaper steel from overseas took away their business. The empty plant stands to this day on the shore.

For boating people, the yacht clubs were landmarks. Just as for golfing people, the golf clubs stood out. It depended on your interests what you noticed. The two oldest churches also stood out, with St. Anne's Chapel on a slight promontory on East River Road and Church Road (a larger Sacred Heart Catholic Church is nearby), and St. James' chapel and church on East River Road near Bellevue Road. The other churches, the Lutheran, Baptist, and Presbyterian, dotted the interior. They had come too late to get riverfront property.

In the south of the island there was what we called the "Wonder Well," a sulfurous spring. A company was drilling for oil in 1903 and instead found mineral water. This mineral water was actually bottled and sold through the 1950s. A small fireworks company set up nearby. The owner got local boys to work for him. My friend, Barry Dixon, who grew up nearby, told me how he and a friend would sneak out late at night and taking a few cracker balls, climb up a tall pine tree near the Wonder Well. It was a common "make-out" place for local teenagers. When Barry and his friend had settled up high in the pine tree, they would throw down a cracker ball at a car below. The young man would jump out of the car and look around. "Who is there?" But he could not see anyone so he would go back in the car. About ten minutes later, the boys in the tall tree would do the same thing with another cracker ball. The people in the car never looked up. It never occurred to them that there were people in the tree.

The Wonder Well finally went dry in 1994. I just remember the awful smell of the area. Sulfur smells like rotten eggs. I don't know how people could imagine it was healthy.

I don't consider the schools landmarks since they kept changing, especially for my class. But I suppose for other people they stood out. Also Macomb Street with its shops was special among island streets.

There were also less visible landmarks, like the supposed arrow-mark on the old house on West River Road. It was the house just to the north of Westcroft Gardens. It had been built by a Rucker in 1848, and sold to the Stantons and their descendants, the deBeaussets, who own it to this day. It is a large two-story house with a front porch running the length of the house. The front door in the middle of the house has a mark on it that everyone said had been made by an arrow. Who was to say? But it was a good story.

For islanders, our own homes were our main landmarks. To come over the bridge, take the road to wherever we lived, that was the best place. That was where we relaxed, knowing we were safe and home on our island.

PART FOUR:

High School on the Island and Beyond

Beginning High School, Botulism, and First Step off the Island

High school now is mostly tenth through twelfth grade, but when we were students it was ninth through twelfth grade. It is a special time in America and is its own society. There are people who are popular and those who are not. For girls in my generation, to be a cheerleader meant certain status. That must have been why I had tried to do a flip in eighth grade that ended with me breaking my leg. I could see the social value in becoming a cheerleader. I certainly had no interest in football games. Looks mattered too and being attractive to boys. For boys it was athletics and getting along with other in-boys. Eventually having a girlfriend probably mattered to them too.

I had always gotten along with my classmates through elementary school and in junior high to a lesser extent. However I was not moving toward a career in popularity in high school. This was not just my inability to do flips and be a cheerleader. I was not fitting in on several fronts. I did not relate to the in-music. Students had gotten hand-held plastic radios in junior high and listened to "popular music." I had been raised on classical music from home. The music the others listened to sounded shallow to me. Also I was not particularly interested in boys. I liked boys, but as friends, nothing more. Don't get me wrong; I wanted to go to the dances. When John Almond asked me to the main dance in ninth grade, I was most pleased. He was a fine person. He had even visited me at home when my leg was in a cast. I remember the bright green dress I wore to the dance with him. But to be honest, I was more interested in my classes.

We had Mrs. Sells again for math. She was as stimulating as ever. I loved algebra. It was like a language and the analysis was fun. We all worked hard in her class. She was the kind of teacher who gave us plenty of homework on weekdays but not on weekends. It was the time of space travel. Mrs. Sells took off one whole class period so we could all follow the trajectory of the latest space satellite on the blackboard. She made learning exciting.

Gym class was better too because we had more field hockey. It was a game with no throwing or silly rules like the limited ones for girls' basketball. With field hockey we had large fields to play in. I played wing, one of the two ends on the offensive front line. I was good at running. Since we no longer had recess we needed this in gym class.

Finally there was French class. I had been wanting to study French for many years. The teacher, Mrs. Stanley, actually knew French and was a good teacher. In eighth grade we had studied Spanish from a strange teacher who stayed only one year with her husband. They both liked Ayn Rand, whom I had never heard of. She also taught us diagramming sentences which made sense to me. But her Spanish was not inspired. I do not think she knew the culture or the language very well. In contrast the ninth grade French teacher was truly fluent and had a Swiss background; her last name was the result of marriage. Little did I know that she would leave after only a few years due to family concerns. That would be the end of good French instruction at Grosse Ile. But while it lasted I was most grateful.

My parents had known of my desire to learn French since I was little and I had memorized French records. One day my father found an advertisement in the back of *Vogue* magazine for a summer French camp in Maine called "École Arcadie." Daddy did not read *Vogue* magazine, but Mom had left it in the bathroom and he happened to look at it from the back and saw the advertisement. He wrote them, telling them he wanted his daughter to go there. They did not respond. So he called them collect. It turned out only students from élite schools in Boston and New York went to this summer French camp. These students had studied French from first grade on. I was from a public school in the Midwest by Detroit. I had only had one year of French in ninth grade.

But before summer, something strange happened on the island. One morning in March as we walked to the bus stop at the end of Colonial Court, we saw there was an emergency vehicle by the Brown's house on the corner. What was going on?

It turned out Mrs. Brown had had a friend, Mrs. McCarthy, over for lunch the day before, another Catholic mother like Mrs. Brown. They had had tuna fish sandwiches from canned tuna. Mrs. Brown's mother who lived with them had come in late and remarked that they had not left any for her. The younger mothers had become ill within a few hours of eating the tuna sandwiches. In thirteen hours Mrs. Brown had died! That is why the emergency vehicle was there. It turned out there had been botulism in the canned tuna. Five days later Mrs. McCarthy died too.

That left nine children without mothers; Mrs. Brown had four children and Mrs. McCarthy had five. Why had this happened? The fabric of families should not be so easily torn. How to cope with such an event? We had no idea.

That summer after ninth grade I went to École Arcadie for six weeks. It was held near Bar Harbor, Maine, in two old mansions on the coast. The girls were housed in one mansion, the boys in the other mansion. The instructors were from France and had spent the previous year teaching at colleges and universities in the United States. We had classes six days a week. The French have no idea of summer camp. For punishment we had to go swimming. The Labrador Current came in there and it was freezing cold.

I was greeted in French and told in French that if I did not speak French I would be *mis à la porte*. I did not know that the phrase meant "kicked out," but I knew it was bad. I had the weakest French of all the students in the entire camp and was put in class "1.A." In the girls' house I was in a room on the second floor with fifteen other young women in bunk beds. One of my roommates was totally fluent in French. I listened a lot. They had put most of the Jewish students on the third floor, which was the hottest. I was meeting Jewish girls my age and anti-Semitism for the first time. We had one Jewish family I knew on the island, the Kaufmans, and they lived near us on Church Road. They had five boys and had moved to Michigan from New Jersey in hopes their sons would go in-state to the University of Michigan.

At École Arcadie one of the Jewish students protested and they moved her down to the second floor. Her name was Abby and we became fast friends. She was from New York City and was dedicated to the theater. Abby and I would write each other letters in French for several years and I visited her in New York City. Later, at a difficult time in my life, she called me every Friday, something that sustained me. She became an actress, but in waiting for auditions for theater positions, she took to drawing and found she like drawing better than acting. She has become a recognized artist as Abby Leigh, her married name, in New York and beyond.

Every evening after dinner at the French camp we sang *La Marseillaise*, the French national anthem, in preparation for the visit of the French ambassador, but then he did not come. Still it was good to have learned it. I can sing it to this day with gusto. The classes were small and focused. I still recall the first book I read in French, *Médecin sous les tropiques*, "Doctor in the Tropics." I had not mastered pronunciation of the French "r." A teacher used to say it to me again and again, almost spitting in my face. On the airplane on the way home, I was suddenly able to pronounce it. I also had to memorize a long fable by LaFontaine. This I did and recited it in public at the end of camp. I had a regular poetry class besides. We had French movies that we watched in the evening in a dark garage with many mosquitoes. I remember one movie where two

French women fought in a laundry and pulled at each other's earrings until the blood flowed in the soapy water. "That's it," I said to myself. "I will never get my ears pierced." I have not had them pierced to this day.

I returned from École Arcadie much stronger in French and more aware of another part of America. Abby and I continued to write each other letters in French. I had the opportunity to get off the island, and so when I did not fit in with island popularity in high school, it still did not feel good. But I knew there was another world out there.

Football,
Harlem Globetrotters,
and Women's Lives

By the next year, I was starting to see what high school was all about and football seemed to be a major part of this. Why this was so, I could not fathom. Perhaps it was because football season was in the fall so it came early in the school year and set the scene. Grosse Ile had not been especially good in football. The surrounding downriver towns like Wyandotte and Trenton had bigger schools and were better in sports. We never played them. We were a "lower class" school when I was a student, which referred to the numbers of students we had. That is, we did not have many students, so we played other schools that did not have many students either. These were mostly farming communities. However the students in the farming communities tended to be better at football than we were. I do not know what it was like for the boys who played football, but it must have been discouraging.

This would change during our high school time and in the future. I did not follow the change and I am not a good source on male sports, which is all there was then. But by our senior year, we had one of the best football teams and were second in the state in our class! For the 1965 football season, we were unbeaten at 9-0. This has not been repeated at Grosse Ile, but we have had good football teams since. In our class there were players like Bob Miltenberger and Ron Solack who continued to play football in college after high school.

There was always hype for the football games. We would gather in the new gym and have rallies, especially before home games. The cheerleaders in their uniforms would lead us in cheers. The school band would play too. The players lined up on the front rows of the gym. This was to get us excited about the upcoming game.

The games were held out in the field in the evening where we played field hockey in gym class. There were bleachers, hard grey metal bleachers. The band came to home games and played. The football players would come running out in their uniforms and shoulder pads and helmets, looking bigger than in real life. The other team would then come running out too, looking even bigger, and their supporters would sit in a section, just somewhat separate from the supporters of our section. I had not mastered the rules of football games. The games seemed endless, especially if it rained. The bleachers were so hard to sit on. The cheerleaders tried to keep us involved. My mind would wander.

There was a special football game known as "Homecoming." People who had graduated from Grosse Ile High School in the past would come back and go to that game. I never did that, but it seemed a nice idea. What was special about the game for students still in high school was the preparation of floats and the election of a queen. Each grade in the high school had to prepare a float. This turned out to be a lot of work and required cooperation. Some years went better than others. The queen would be elected from the senior class and was a big deal. I did not follow it much until my senior year. The four young women in contention would be driven around the island on the backs of convertibles the afternoon of the game, and then around the field before the game. At some point in the evening, the name of the queen would be announced, and she would be driven around the football field with a crown on her head. The floats would be there too and there was a competition for the best float.

Besides Homecoming, I do remember another game that got some attention. We had a big Catholic family named Kuhn. Dr. Kuhn had nine or ten children. The boys all played football. At one football game, at some point some island supporter yelled, "Go Kuhn!" Unfortunately there was a Black player on the other side. This caused problems and the game stopped. Why were we making fun of the Black player? They thought we were calling him a negative term. We had to explain that our player's name was Kuhn. It took some time before they believed us.

One of the advantages of high school was that we now had our Roman Catholic neighbors back in school with us. They had been in kindergarten with us. Then most of them had gone to the Catholic school on the island for first through eighth grade. They rejoined us for high school in ninth grade. Those of us who had been together all through elementary and junior high knew each other almost too well by this time so we were ready for new blood by ninth grade. These were not just those who had been with us in kindergarten. There were also new Catholic students who had moved to the island in the interim and lived in the new developments of Potawatomi Woods and other new areas. A few Catholic students went off-island to Catholic high schools, but most joined us for high school in the public school.

Tenth grade however was not a good year for me in mathematics. The wonderful Mrs. Sells took a year's sabbatical and I had Mrs. Meagher for geometry. I liked Mrs. Meagher. She was an islander and sang German songs for us at Christmas. But geometry was on the second floor of the high school and my seat that year was next to the window. I could look out at the river, watch the freighters go by, and see across to Canada. The combination of missing Mrs. Sells, and the pull of the river-scape meant I did not focus on geometry the way I should have. If I wanted to build bridges like the Ambassador Bridge, I needed to do well in geometry. I much preferred algebra. Was it the teacher? Was it where I sat? I got good grades, but I never learned geometry the way I should have.

Mr. Appleyard taught us English. He was mostly a good teacher, although he never had us write papers. As I reflect on this I realize he did not want to bother to correct them. This would have taken a lot of time. People only learn to write by writing. When I became a professor, years later, I always had students write two-page papers every week. They needed to write regularly to learn how to write. And I had them write eight- to fifteen-page research papers in all my classes. Yes it took time to respond to student papers, but as a teacher, that was my job.

That year in Mr. Appleyard's class, I read the book *Cry the Beloved Country* (1948), by Alan Paton, a South African writer who was under house arrest. We had to read a book of our choice, a good assignment. I learned of the book by Paton thanks to my mother. After I read it I decided to write to Alan Paton. But since he was under house arrest, his wife answered me. I was so excited to receive a letter from South Africa. This was the beginning of the Civil Rights era in America but apartheid was rampant in South Africa. We had a long way to go in America. And South Africa had a long way to go too. From reading Paton's book, I began to follow events in South Africa. I remember when the leader Steve Biko was killed in 1977 by government police. I later read biographies of Nelson Mandela and was impressed that he had not become embittered after twenty-seven years of imprisonment. He gardened and also made his bed as a form of discipline. When I make my bed to this day, I think of Mandela. I remember too when Mandela came to Detroit and spoke in Tiger Stadium in 1990. He said, "We worked so hard for the vote. Why do you not all vote?"

My sophomore year was also the spring that the Harlem Globetrotters came to Grosse Ile High School and put on an exhibition game. Most of us had never heard of the Harlem Globetrotters before and we all went to see them play in our gymnasium. They were phenomenal.

The Harlem Globetrotters played basketball in ways we had never seen before. They were so fast and they made shots that we had never seen. Remember this was before players made three-pointers. The Globetrotters made three-pointers. They were funny too. But their skill was so apparent in passing, in dribbling, and in their overall team coordination. On top of this they were all Black. This was new for Grosse Ile.

I later learned that the Globetrotters were originally not from New York at all. They were from Illinois and had begun in the 1920s. They had a manager who thought that a New York-type name would be more exotic and since Harlem was the cultural capital of Black people, it was a natural name for them. In 1940 the Harlem Globetrotters beat a white national basketball champion team. Later they added the comic element. They played all over the country, and then all over the world.

I have no idea what the Globetrotters thought of our little island. But we were mightily impressed with them. I like to think that they helped open our eyes to a bigger world in sports and in race.

On a more mundane level, babysitting was part of my island education. There were not many ways to earn money on the island and especially not many for girls. Babysitting was one way.

People do not realize what babysitters see about a family's life. I recall the first time a saw an expensive magazine with a woman on the cover holding only a bouquet of flowers in front of her pubic area. "Miss September" she was called. I went home and described this to my parents. I had seen my first *Playboy* magazine. It seemed ironic to me since the family did not pay me well but the magazine was clearly expensive. I knew nothing about pornography or its more élite forms.

This was an era when people were meant to get married and have children. There was talk of people playing around but then it was denied or pushed under the carpet. I never heard of anyone on the island getting a divorce.

One family I babysat for was a family that lived close to us. The wife was from Detroit but she had married an island man. She had a university degree in English and journalism, and had worked downtown for Hudson's Department store in a good job before she married. Why she had married her husband I never knew. He had flunked out of university the first year and never amounted to much. He had a good tenor voice. That was it. They had several children right off—before birth control. The mother was always cutting out coupons to pay for food. The father played around and kept a non-working sports car, a Triumph, in the garage. After a while he would only come home to have her do his laundry. When she inherited some money, she gave it to him and he spent it. That was after my babysitting time. Why did she not kick him out for good? I guess people did not think that way then, but I would not have done his laundry or given him a dime.

Was being married that important? It was a different world. Women's groups did not exist on the island and there were few options for work there either. The mother of this unfortunate couple wrote occasionally for the island paper, *The Ile Camera*. I do not think it paid much.

Much later when I applied for my divorce, my mother did not support me, saying there had not been a divorce in our family. This was patently untrue since my oldest aunt had been divorced. But my father did support me and so did my grandmother. Even among my own generation though I noticed how married women avoided me and were afraid I would steal their husbands. I wanted to tell them that wild horses could not make me interested in their husbands. The worst ones were those who themselves wanted out of marriages but were too afraid to take action. So even later it was not easy being divorced. And some men thought you were an easy mark. Still it was better than staying with a man like the father of that family.

But in the 1960s on the island, women had not reached the point where they stood up for themselves, let alone got out of bad marriages. They coped, sometimes with depression and alcohol. Women blamed themselves for problems. They were supposed to make everything work, no matter. And some of the men did not have it so easy either. The business world was high-powered and heartless. When a man who had worked for the Ford Motor Company all his career was let go, he lost his identity. He could easily take to drink too.

I later wondered after my own divorce, if the island had prepared me emotionally for relationships. We did not talk about emotions. So much was unspoken. I am sure this varied by families. And yet I think we were emotionally reticent. Our values of hard work and persistence carried us through, whatever happened, but did not necessarily make us good judges of character. We could be surprised by people who did not share our values.

Frog Dissection, *Silent Spring*, Large Lake Research Station

Tenth grade was also the year we took biology. When the biology teacher entered our classroom at eight o'clock in the morning for first period, he would announce, "Daylight in the swamp." My older sister told me he had said the same thing at the beginning of her biology class too. He was a tall man and also coached basketball. I would have thought that biology would have been a popular course on the Island. We had grown up outside and liked plants, trees, and animals. But it was not a popular class.

What I remember most about my experience in biology was the teacher's response to my dissection of a frog. I liked frogs. I liked how they moved and their colors. I did not like the idea of cutting up a frog. But we had no choice, so I did what we had to do. After we completed our dissections, we had to display them in a sort of open framed box, label the parts, and bring this up to the teacher for examination. When I brought up my labeled dissection in the box, the teacher, who knew I was a good student, looked down at me from his height and said, "That is the worst dissection of a frog I have ever seen." He did not tell me what was wrong or how to improve. Just that it was very poorly done. I went back to my seat, mortified. I looked over at my classmates' dissections. They were not that different from mine. Then I looked up at the teacher. He was just being cruel. But I never forgot what the biology teacher had said to me. And I never took another biology course.

My father had said part of life is getting along with bad teachers. But cruel teachers are another matter. I am sure I was not his only target. I wonder how many other students over his career he said cutting things to. The principal then was Mr. Gingrich, a mathematics teacher. Undoubtedly the biology teacher behaved differently in front of him. I later heard the biology teacher resented the students on the island. Then he should not have been teaching there.

Overall I think the students on the island were a good group of students. People on the island valued education. In my high school class of 150 students, there was only one student whose graduation was in question. Most of us went on to college. And this has continued. In recent times, there has even been a robotics team that has done well nationally. Back in the 1960s, with the island's physical setting, its marshes and wildlife, and students' interest in the outdoors, it should have been an easy place to make biology a popular subject.

In addition, this was a time when the importance of nature was coming into the public sphere. There had been a series of articles over the summer in *The New Yorker* that were published as a book to great acclaim in September, 1962. I refer to the *Silent Spring* by Rachel Carson. It woke people up about environmental issues. Rachel Carson had written less controversial books earlier about the sea, like *The Sea Around Us*. But the new book, *Silent Spring*, was very different. In it Rachel Carson showed how synthetic pesticides like DDT, when they came into the biosphere, not only killed bugs, but also went up the food chain to other animals including children. If we poisoned nature, we would poison people. She made it understandable to the general public. My parents and their friends on the island talked about it. Eventually this would lead to modern ecology.

There was backlash to Rachel Carson as the companies that made the pesticides fought back. But she had powerful people on her side, including President Kennedy who established a presidential committee to investigate pesticides. Rachel Carson was especially against aerial spraying.

How did questions of chemical poisons affect the Island? Remember Grosse Ile is downriver from Detroit, with manufacturing and chemical plants along its shoreline. Pollution was not new to us. My father had been going to pollution meetings for quite a while.

Once when a cousin of mine came to the Island, we took a long walk to the north end of the Island where there was a lot of white waste. We walked out on the hills of this sludge-like material. When we got home and my father found out where we had been, he was furious. His company of Wyandotte Chemicals owned the rights to the land on this part of the Island and had used it for dumping. It became clear that they had dumped pollutants there. We were told never to go there again.

So when my father went to pollution meetings, as a chemist he understood what had been going on. Earlier in the 1940s and 1950s, companies had dumped materials without regard for how it affected the surrounding areas. Finally people were beginning to realize the severity of the problems this could cause with the build-up over the years.

The Detroit area had its experience of pollutants of water, land, and air. There was a time in 1948 when 11,000 ducks had died by the community of River Rouge, north of us closer to Detroit, due to an oil spill on the water. Millions of gallons of oil were being dumped untreated into the river each year. It could pollute the whole western basin of Lake Erie. The air quality, from the energy and manufacturing plants in Detroit, was such that Detroit had double the percentage of cases of asthma of any other place in Michigan.

The river that flowed past the Island got water pollution from Detroit and from the more northern downriver communities. It also got air pollution from McClouth Steel across the river.

By the 1960s the Water Pollution Control Administration described the Detroit River as "one of the most polluted rivers" in the United States. They even opened a sort of laboratory—a Large Lakes Research Station—on Grosse Ile to monitor environmental quality. As students we would have been fascinated to know about this. I only learned about it much later. But perhaps people on the Island who knew about the Research Station did not want to publicize how bad the Detroit River actually was.

In 1965 the quality of water in Lake Erie was such that some characterized Lake Erie as "dying from pollution." Much of this was phosphorus-induced algae blooms. Where there were beaches along the lakeshore they sometimes had to bring in bulldozers to take out the decomposing algae and dead fish. Lake Erie got pollution not just from the urban centers of Detroit and Cleveland, but also from fertilizers of all the agricultural lands whose runoff dumped into rivers that fed into the lake. These include agricultural lands in southwest Ontario and northwest Ohio that contributed much sediment to the lake. Compared to other Great Lakes, the Lake Erie watershed is the most populated of the Great Lakes basins. It is exposed to the greatest stress from urbanization, industrialization, and agriculture. It is also the shallowest of the Great Lakes. Islanders who lived at the south end of the island were most aware of these problems.

The pollution problems at this time were not just in the Great Lakes. In the 1960s in other parts of the United States there were a series of pollution events. In New York City over Thanksgiving in 1966 there were three days of extreme air pollution known as smog. There were several large oil spills on both coasts. Most famous was when the Cuyahoga River caught fire south of Cleveland in June, 1969, with flames that burned for half an hour.

These events, along with the growing concerns over pollution in many river systems that had been brewing since *Silent Spring*, led to the founding of the EPA, the Environmental Protection Agency, in 1970. Before this air pollution, water, waste management, pesticide research, and other environmental programs had all been spread across several departments of the federal government. With the EPA they would be under a single agency so monitoring and protection could be coordinated.

In 1972 the Clean Water Act and the Canada-United States Great Lakes Water Quality Agreement were passed. The environmental problems of the Detroit River had helped provide a major rationale for the Clean Water Act. This Act set up programs to determine standards that needed to be met for pollution prevention, water quality, and monitoring.

Lake Erie got significant attention with the Canada-United States Great Lakes Water Quality Agreement. It dealt seriously with the amount of phosphorus in Lake Erie and the water quality got much better. Unfortunately in the twenty-first century there are new problems with algae. We do not know what is causing it now. Hopefully it will be determined and dealt with.

As for the Detroit River, it is now significantly cleaner thanks to significant reduction of pollution since the Clean Water Act went into effect. These reductions include: over 97% reduction in oil releases, 90% decrease in phosphorus discharges, 4,600 tons/day decrease in chloride discharges, upgrading of wastewater treatment plants, 80% reduction in untreated waste, 85% reduction in mercury in fish, 90% reduction in PCBs in herring gull eggs, and remediation of one million cubic yards of contaminated sediment.

In the late 1980s zebra mussels entered the Great Lakes from ballast in foreign ships. Zebra mussels are able to filter water and while they have had negative effects on the fishing industry since they feed on basic nutrients, in Lake Erie they actually helped the Clean Water Act in improving the quality of the water. The addition of holding tanks on freighters and private boats also helped clean up the Great Lakes so sewage was not flushed into the water but had to be pumped out and disposed of elsewhere.

Besides reductions in chemicals in the water, the changes in wildlife are another sign of improvements. Birds like bald eagles and peregrine falcons, that had not been seen in years due to the pesticides, have come back. Fish, including lake sturgeon, lake whitefish, and walleye, have also returned. Even some beaver have been seen. They had been hunted out by the fur trade long ago so it is remarkable that some have come back.

When President Kennedy was Shot

A major event during our high school years was the killing of President Kennedy. Many people can remember where they were on November 22, 1963, when they heard the terrible news. My friends who went to Catholic high schools tell me this was an even bigger event there because Kennedy was the first Catholic president. But it affected Americans of all religions all over the country including on the island.

I was in the car with my mother in the parking lot of the island school. It was early afternoon. We had just come back from some appointment when we heard the news on the radio of the shooting of the President in Texas. We could not believe it. We just sat there in the corner of the parking lot and listened again. Dallas, Texas. What was President Kennedy doing there? In an open motorcade, they said, with Mrs. Kennedy next to him. And Governor Connelly of Texas in the front seat, also shot. Was the president at the hospital? Oh no. They said he had been pronounced dead! The president had been shot and killed in Texas. It was about 2 o'clock in the afternoon in Michigan.

I did not want to go back to school. But our classes went to 3:30. So I said goodbye to my mother and went back to tenth grade geometry class. I went up to the second floor. All was quiet. They had all heard the news. What could anyone say? Some of the teachers had cried when they first got the news. Even the difficult biology teacher who coached basketball and who people said had wanted to be a doctor, who took out his frustrations on students, he had cried.

We went home on the school buses and heard from our parents and neighbors where they had been when they heard the news. Some schools and businesses had closed right away. Flags were at half-mast. The country was in mourning. How had this been allowed to happen?

No one knew how to cope or what to do. All we could do was listen to the radio. We learned that they had taken the president's body back to Air Force One at the Dallas Airport. There, with Mrs. Kennedy beside him, on Air Force One, the Vice-President, Lyndon Baines Johnson, had taken the oath of office to become president of the United States. Then they had flown back to Washington. Kennedy had been president for less than three years. It had gone so fast. None of us could have expected this.

We all later saw photographs of Jackie Kennedy in her pink suit with pink hat, before the shooting, sitting next to her husband in the open car as it traveled through Dallas. And then afterward, there she was with blood on her suit, standing next to LBJ as he took the oath of office.

We learned that Lee Harvey Oswald, an American and former marine, was arrested that night for the shooting. He had shot the president once in the neck and twice in the head with a rifle from a nearby building as the motorcade passed by. But why? Oswald had lived in Russia and had a Russian wife. But we never found out the reason because two days later, a nightclub owner, Jack Ruby, shot and killed Lee Harvey Oswald in the garage of the Dallas police station as they were taking him to the county jail.

President Kennedy's funeral procession was beautiful to watch as the coffin moved along the streets of the capital city. Little John Kennedy saluted. Did he understand what had happened? How could he.

President Kennedy had been special. He was young, only forty-three when he was elected in 1960. But he was perceived as even younger since he contrasted so with Eisenhower, the previous president. He also had a younger wife. Jackie was twelve years younger than he was. And their children were very young as well. His youth caught the attention of people across the country.

At Kennedy's inauguration, he didn't wear a hat. That was said to have changed the fashion in men's headwear; they no longer wore hats the way they had in the past. Also Robert Frost read a poem at his inauguration. But most important in his inaugural address were his famous words, "Ask not what your country can do for you, but what you can do for your country." Those of us in Michigan related this to the Peace Corps which he had earlier announced from the steps of the Michigan Union in Ann Arbor when he was still campaigning in the fall of 1960.

President Kennedy's wife had been a special first lady. She too was younger than any other first ladies in recent memory. She was very attractive and knew how to dress. There was the sadness with the babies she lost. What stood out in people's minds especially was the televised tour of the White House that she led. Apparently she had found the White House in poor condition when she moved in. She had an almost breathy way of talking that made you want to follow her as she led you around the rooms. We heard too, via her husband, how well she was treated when they went to France because she spoke French. They were indeed a handsome couple. What we did not hear, at that time, was his behind-the-scenes carousing.

Kennedy became president at a difficult time in the Cold War. As I learned when I went to France, he had increased advisors to South Vietnam. He had tense relations with the Soviet Union. There was the Bay of Pigs incident in Cuba, followed by the more serious Cuban Missile Crisis. Lyndon Baines Johnson was his vice-president, and his trip to Texas in November of 1963 was partly to work to secure Texas for the Democrats in the next election.

For many of us the assassination of President Kennedy was a sign of how unpredictable life could be. We hadn't been involved in politics. But such an event had been unthinkable. The Civil Rights Movement was in full force, but it was mostly in the South at that time. The Vietnam War would later call up many young men of our generation and go on for years to no discernible purpose. The 1960s were a time of change, and as we became involved, we realized that America needed to change. President Kennedy, had he lived, would have had to change too. I wish he had had the opportunity to grow.

Summer in France:
Second Step off the Island

My first step off the island had been to French camp in Maine. There I had met people from New York, New England, and France. They made me aware of a much wider world. When I had gone to camp in Canada it had not felt that different, more like a continuation of my island home but of an earlier time.

Since I was young I had wanted to travel. When I was seven, I remembered climbing to the top of the old oak tree in the field behind our house, and vowing that I would get beyond Meridian, the farthest road I could see that ran north and south through the Island. Later I wrote to steamship companies and asked for posters which I then put up on the walls of my bedroom. I had a great uncle from Detroit who had traveled around the world in the nineteenth century. I had an engraved ostrich shell from his travels. Unfortunately he had also gotten a "social disease" during his travels that I imagine was syphilis. Truly travel involves different kinds of learning.

My second step off the island I took after tenth grade when I went by ship to France for eight weeks in the summer. It was the junior program of Experiment in International Living out of Vermont. Again I think it was my father who found the program. My parents drove me to the ship in New York and we stopped at their friends' house in New Jersey. The friends thought I was attractive in an unusual way. This was something new for me. No one had ever said that before. My braces were off. I was fifteen and had dark thick hair and very fair skin. I did not believe them. Northern New Jersey reminded me of downriver Detroit with all the chemical smells.

My parents dropped me off at the ship in the harbor of New York. The ship was an old Italian one that took immigrants from the Mediterranean to Australia in the winter, and students from New York to Europe in the summer. This was before there were many planes that took students to Europe. On the ship it was chaotic in that people could not find their right cabins. The signs for the decks were color words in Italian while our tickets were all in English. I was supposed to be on Blue Deck, but in Italian that is *azzurro*. Most people did not know Italian so it took a long time to get people on the right deck, let alone the right cabin, each with bunk beds. It was good that I was with the seven other girls from my group. Our group also included eight boys. We were the youngest people on the ship. Most were college students.

It took us eight days to cross the Atlantic. That is a long time and the food was not good. The soup was tasteless. I gained new respect for the ocean. They showed movies down below. I remember "Loneliness of the Long-Distance Runner." I was happy when we finally reached Le Havre on the northern coast of France. I even remember seeing a young man who met the ship in an old army jacket. His girlfriend on the ship threw him down a roll before we were fully landed.

But in the first restaurant we went to for lunch, when I asked for the bathroom in French, they announced they did not have one. They could not be that different! It turned out I needed to ask for the "W.C." in French — from the British for "water closet." That is what they had, not a room with a bath. I would learn quickly and my spoken French was among the best in the group thanks to my time at École Arcadie.

They drove us to Mont Saint-Michel the next day but it was full of tourists so we didn't go onto the island. Fortunately we were staying nearby so we were able to see Mont Saint-Michel in early evening light. It is just off the coast and was beautiful with the stone towers of the medieval abbey and monastery rising out of the sea against the sky. We then walked around the small island through the narrow streets, quieted by its loveliness.

Mont Saint-Michel in the early evening. Photo by F. Trix.

The first place we stayed several days was Brittany. Minority regions of countries are often the most interesting. I bought a bracelet with old Breton symbols on it that I still have. I also bought a blue notebook. My mother had told me to keep a diary that I wrote in every day. Between the diary writing and the letters home, my memories of time in France were made stronger. Later I would realize it was this summer that I learned to write. My mother even saved my letters. I also realized that my mother had never had such an experience when she was young. She was the sixth of seven children and the Depression had hit Detroit hard. Her father had lost all his money twice. I was most fortunate to be able to travel like this at age fifteen.

There was a strike and the farmers dumped cartloads of artichokes in the road. There was also a national parade for July 14, Bastille Day. I remember many older men in uniforms, some very old ones with beards who must have been from the First World War,

Bastille Day parade in Plouescat, Brittany, France. Photo by F. Trix.

marching through the streets of the small Breton town of Plouescat.

We stayed in a boarding school that was fine with me since I had lived in dormitories at camp. Others found it more difficult.

Slowly I was getting to know the others in our group. They were from different regions of America. Several were there because their parents were getting a divorce. One was there because her twin brother had recently died and she was grieving. Others had academic issues. One was going off to college the next year. I was one of the few who was mainly drawn to the French language and culture. Later I would learn this trip was ammunition against my grandmother who had wanted to send me away to boarding school.

Next we visited the Loire region of France with all its castles and historic sites. In the evening we would attend *son et lumière* presentations, that is, "sound and light" shows that would tell the history of the chateau through music and light playing on different parts of the chateau. It was most effective and made the history of the chateau come alive.

We also had two leaders: a middle-aged woman, Jean, a French teacher at a respected girls' school in the East who was most knowledgeable, and a younger man, David, who was of French descent. The male leader told the boys early on to watch out for the girls in our group since French men liked younger women. I had begun to notice that the French men were looking at me much more than this ever happened in America.

We took a night train down from Paris to the South. The south of France has a totally different feel from the north. We were supposed to stay with separate

Frances in central France.

families for a week, after which the young people in the families would go to the Riviera with us for five days. I ended up with a family in Aix-en-Provence who were *Pied-Noir* or "Black-Foot." That signifies they were people of European origin, mostly French, who had been born in Algeria during the period of French rule. They were angry with de Gaulle for making them leave North Africa and return to France. We watched a news conference with de Gaulle on television, totally controlled by de Gaulle. At the end, the five-year old in the family said, *"Tais-tois de Gaulle,"* "Shut up, de Gaulle." He had used the familiar form, totally irreverent. With this family I had yogurt for the first time. I thought it was ice cream until I tasted it. Little did I know I would come to love yogurt when I lived in Turkey much later in my life. They also had an older dark-haired cousin, Danielle, staying with them from the north of France.

Then we went to the Riveria. The Mediterranean is memorable with its palms, beaches, and blue waters. Danielle and I roomed together in a tent and I taught her how to shave her legs. But what I remember best about the time on the Mediterranean was hearing Ella Fitzgerald sing an outside concert. She sang out over beach crowds who clearly knew enough to appreciate what they were hearing. We did not have tickets, but we listened just the same, lying back, and hearing "Summertime," sung as only Ella could, across the Mediterranean shore.

From the Mediterrean, we said goodbye to the family members we had stayed with in Aix and the Riveria, and journeyed north to Avignon where we walked up on the famous bridge, but you could not cross it—it was not connected. Then to Geneva and Chamonix in the Alps where I spent my sixteenth birthday and bought myself a light blue sweater. Blue was still my favorite color. While we were in the mountains I went up on a hillside to write in my diary and met an older man who told me what it was like being in Europe during the Nazi times. He had barely escaped with his life. World War II was still very alive in the early 1960s in France. There were many war memorials, especially in the North. I sometimes wondered how many of them were true. In occupied Vichy France it had been hard to resist the Germans.

Later that week I was sitting near Jean, the female leader of our group, when news came that America was sending more advisors to Vietnam. I knew nothing about Vietnam. But Jean exclaimed in horror, "This is just the beginning!" She had known what had happened to the French when they had been in Vietnam.

We took the train back to Paris. On the train I met a Black man who spoke good French. He must have seen my astonishment. He laughed in my face. I only knew Black people in Detroit but none spoke French. My world was expanding and it needed to.

The first day in Paris I walked all over the city. The second day I discovered the Metro—the subway—and after that I could get anywhere. I liked the way they had the same advertisement repeated all along the wall, so you saw *la vache qui rit*, "the laughing cow" cheese ad with the head of the big red cow, many times as the subway sped past.

We discovered the museum of impressionist artists, *Le Jeu de Paume*, when it was still in its own smaller building. We spent hours there. And one morning we got up early and all went to the old Paris market, *Les Halles*, where we had hot onion soup with cheese on top. They were wise to leave Paris for the end when we were more able to get around ourselves. I even remember being in a cheese shop where I was buying cheese as a gift for my grandparents and the manager came over to ask my help. Imagine, asking the help of a teenage American girl. The manager could not understand another foreigner. So I went over to help. The foreigner was not an American. I listened to what the man wanted. He said in a deeply accented voice several times, something like "got, got." "Ahh," I said. *"Il veut fromage de chevre."* He wants goat cheese. I had figured it out.

The hotel we stayed in had seen better days. At the end of our stay there one of the other girls ratted up my hair, another had me dress in her black nightgown, I put on orange lipstick, and for fun they took photos of me leaning against the torn wallpaper to show their parents how one of our group looked like "a lady of the night." Things had changed. Indeed a man had tried to get me into a tent in the South but I had gotten out of it. We had matured over the summer. When men said things to me like, "your eyes are like the stars in the sky," I knew how to jokingly respond. By the time we were in Paris, I had a stronger sense of myself.

Our trip back to America was by airplane, not by ship. But it was Icelandic Airlines and twenty-three hours long. We stopped in Reykjavik. I could still spell it from fourth grade on Grosse Ile. We also stopped in Goose Bay, Labrador. It was a propeller plane. The cheese I had bought for my grandparents started to smell. I got home finally. It was a good summer.

I even had trouble adjusting back to the island. I missed the people of our group, the camraderie and the way we could talk with each other. We had an openess that I did not have with people on the island. I realized we had been able to express feelings that we did not express at home. All of a sudden the island seemed a lonely place to me. And for the first time people had told me I was attractive. It had felt good. I needed to connect the two worlds, of the summer group and life at home. But like the bridge of Avignon, they were not easy to connect.

I had taken photographs throughout my trip with an old Voightländer camera but had developed only the first ones in France. I had saved all the rest to be developed back in Michigan. When I went in anticipation to the store in Wyandotte to get my developed photos from France, I found that someone had inadvertently ruined them all. Instead they gave me new rolls of film, with apologies.

That fall I had my first seizure. I do not know why it began then. I was diagnosed with epilepsy. So I would begin taking medication for life. I would not be able to drink alcohol ever again if I wanted the anti-seizure medication to work. Such is life. But I had had a wonderful summer in France.

Neurologists, Writing, and Drivers' Education

Eleventh grade is a comfortable year in high school because you finally know what you are doing and you have a whole year before you have to start thinking about major change. It was a good year for me. I came back from France and sitting near me in study hall was someone whose last name, like mine, was at the end of the alphabet. I did not know him since he had gone to the Catholic school for elementary and lived in Potawatomi Woods. We got to talking and that is how I met Walt Wheeler. Eventually he asked me out. If I had not just been in France I do not think it would have worked out, but I was more confident so it did. Walt was an amateur radio operator and he was fun to talk to.

One day Walt showed up at my house at the end of the gravel court on a light green motorcycle and proudly asked if I wanted a ride. My father came out of the house. He took one look at the motorcycle and asked, "Do you have a helmet for her?" Walt shook his head and slowly headed back the way he had come. Motorcycle rides ended for me before they began.

I was sixteen and so this was the time for Drivers' Education. On Saturday mornings we had classes with films and lectures on driving and safety at the high school. I rode my bike all the way there and back. Early on it became clear that a main purpose of Drivers' Ed. was to scare us so much that we would be careful once we got behind the wheel. The films included some that introduced you to people who then died. We actually knew islanders who had died in car accidents. I remember the older sister of a former babysitter who had been out with three other islanders driving in Trenton one night. They got stuck on a railroad track and were hit by a train. All died except the driver. I always wondered how he felt. It must have been terrible. The whole school and island mourned. But the immediacy of the films worked. We were terrified.

My seizures came along part way through the fall. They were going to put off actual driving for a while I realized. But I would keep taking the classes part. I did not tell anyone about my seizures. It is not something people talked about. But it did begin my meetings with a new class of specialists—neurologists. They are not among my favorite people. Their assistants administer brain wave tests and then the specialists tell you your tests are not normal. They have no idea what seizures are like since have never had them themselves. My notion is a seizure is like a fuse blowing. Neurologists over-prescribe medication to make sure you will not have any more seizures. You also will not have a life. I soon found I could do with only one of the two prescribed drugs. Also "therapeutic level" is a general level, so I worked to keep my medication level as low as possible. Through my life I only had two neurologists who were curious as to why I had seizures and they were both women.

School was good in eleventh grade. No doubt the new confidence I had gained over the summer in France helped. But classes were good too. Mrs. Sells was back so math class was as stimulating as ever. And Mr. Appleyard took us to plays in Detroit at the Hillberry Theater by Wayne State University. We loved going to see the Shakespeare plays that we had read. The theater was not big so we felt enclosed by it. Especially when the knights came running down the aisles from both sides toward the stage, we were entranced. It is the way Shakespeare is meant to be performed.

I had Mr. Parkhurst for world history. He cared about wars too. I read Churchill's *History of the English Speaking People* for his class as an extra book. In economics we also had a good teacher, Mr. Robertson. His idea was that the island should declare itself independent and non-aligned. And then we should solicit aid from both the capitalist and the communist blocks so that we could fix our roads. They were truly awful. The tax base on the island was too low for basic infrastructure. We did not mind not having a swimming pool at the school. But roads were another matter. We did need better roads.

In an American literature class I wrote papers that my mother read. She never criticized my teachers. But she did not trust them, I could tell. She told me my sentences were too long. In one paper I wrote the sentence, "So does Thoreau." With that sentence my mother announced, "Now you can begin to lengthen your sentences." I never forgot that. Over the past summer with all the diary writing and letter writing from France, I must have gotten better at writing in general. I am grateful to my mother for her encouragement in writing and patience in reading my papers. It has served me well my whole life.

I wonder what my mother would have written if someone had encouraged her? She knew how to write and would write verse for friends' occasions. She had an incisive mind and when she described something, we all remembered it that way. Years later, we came home from a dinner down South and she noticed a convocation of wood storks, tall birds with spindly legs standing out in the tidal pool with their wings hunched up to their necks. "Like the burghers of Calais," she said. It was perfect.

We had a special guest come to the high school that year who spoke in the library on the poetry of Walt Whitman. He had no shells or false promises. I had never noticed the poetry of Walt Whitman before. But this man was devoted to him. That is what I remember about the presentation, the devotion more than the actual poetry. It has made me pay more attention to Whitman, his work and his life ever since. Whitman did live at the crucial time around the Civil War. Some lines from "When Lilacs Last in the Dooryard Bloomed," stay with me. No one knew how to cope with President Lincoln's death. We needed poets then.

In the high school library there were some books that were held back from students and required a parent's permission before we could take them out. We presumed they had too many references to sex in them. The librarian was an islander from Hickory Island, and somewhat humorless. I remember when the library needed some new shelves. The workmen came into the library. The librarian announced to them, "Don't make any noise or any mess." They just stood there astounded. One day a senior high school student took the key to the library and went down to the river and threw it in. The librarian was furious.

I finally got permission to take the driving part of Drivers' Ed. when it was ascertained that my anti-seizure medicine was working. But by then all the regular groups had been assigned. I was put with the leftovers. There was a blond boy who was new to the school and was very shy. There was a Polish-American girl from Buffalo. And there was an Iraqi girl who had just come from Philadelphia. She spoke Black English and Arabic. The teacher did not teach in the Grosse Ile system; he taught Drivers' Ed. for extra money. He thought I looked like Katharine Hepburn whom I vaguely knew was a movie actress. I had never seen her in a movie. Remember, we had no theater on the island and video had not come yet.

The Drivers' Ed. teacher had a special car with an extra stopping mechanism where he sat next to the driver. That probably saved our lives several times. My problem was stop signs. I would focus on the road and miss the stop signs. I also had trouble changing speeds going from the highway to the regular roads. I would get used to a certain speed. The Polish-American girl was the best driver. I learned some Polish from her. I think she had driven before. The Iraqi girl was well-meaning but she missed Iraq and she missed Philadelphia too. She had had too many changes in her life. The worst driver was the shy boy. He almost killed us all one day near the steel plant in Trenton. He finally said he could not see where the side of the road was. The teacher exploded and insisted he get his eyes tested. It turned out he needed glasses.

One day when we were doing better than usual, we stopped at a fast food place. These were just coming in and the teacher liked them. We got French fries and the teacher got a shake. Then we took off. Wouldn't you know, on the next street, I don't remember who was driving, but they did a fast stop and the shake went into the teacher's lap. Still I must give him credit. Somehow we all passed and he had figured out that the boy needed his eyes tested before we were all killed.

Later in the year I broke up with my first boyfriend. I remember one morning before a science class he told me he thought I had hairy arms. I looked down at my forearms. Indeed there was hair on them, but not that much. I thought that he could have said many worse things. I was not deeply hurt. We must have been moving apart for a while. He started going out with a girl in a lower grade.

Another boy, whom I did not know well and who had not been on the island long, told me he would ask me out if I got a "D" on a history test. I just looked at him. I did not answer him. But the thought was ridiculous to me. First, why would he think I wanted to go out with him? And second what did my grades have to do with it? I was not aware of male competition. Later in my career I would meet male competition aplenty.

Frances in eleventh grade.

Practical Courses and What We Missed

In eighth grade, all the girls had to take a full year of cooking and sewing in Home Economics, while the boys had to take Shop. In high school there was only one term of a required course for everyone and it was a course on public speaking, known as "Speech." It was not popular. Apart from the priest and the pastors in churches, and the teachers in school, there was not much public speaking on the island. We already knew what people thought. Why embarrass them by having them get up in front of people?

It must have been difficult to teach. There we all sat, silently watching the teacher as she became more animated in attempt to involve us. No, we were not interested in speaking in public. No one could see the point. It seemed a cruel exercise. But at least there was a sort of structure to it. We were supposed to first give an introduction. Something light would be good. Then we should go through the substance of our speech. At the end we needed to conclude to make sure people had understood our point.

At least we tried to follow the model. We spoke quickly to get through it. Or we forgot entirely what we going to say. In our hands we had notes on three-by-five cards. But they were hard to read once we got in front of the class. We could feel each other's embarrassment and we couldn't wait for the period to be over. The upshot was most people vowed not to speak in public if they could avoid it at all costs.

A more positive practical course was typing. This was not required, but it was offered during the year if you had time or as an early short summer course. My mother suggested I take it one summer so I took the short summer course. My mother did not know how to type. In her generation, only people who wanted to become secretaries took typing. But Mom must have seen that there was more value to it than that. I am forever grateful to her. This was before computers. Knowing how to type certainly helped when computers came in twenty years later. But I used typing much before that.

I do not remember much about the typing course. We were introduced to the keyboard layout and how to use our fingers the most efficient way. Then we practiced. The typing machines were in rows and were old manual typewriters. You had to use some pressure to make the keys push down, not the soft touch that later worked on electric typewriters, or that we use on computers nowadays.

I do remember going home after the first lesson and my father, who typed with four fingers, telling me to type, "The quick brown fox jumps over the lazy dog." Apparently this sentence uses all the letters of the alphabet. I used to practice by typing what people were saying on my thighs as they spoke. It must have looked strange, but it kept me practicing. I couldn't check accuracy though.

When I went off to college, many of our papers needed to be typed. I was so grateful that I could type. People who couldn't type had to pay people to type for them. And one summer I made extra money typing out lessons in Spanish. I never learned Spanish, but the patterns were not difficult.

My father got into computers early and later went with me in 1985 to help me get a computer. I wanted an Apple because it had the alphabets for different languages but it didn't have enough memory then so I got a PC. Again it was crucial that I could type. I typed my own dissertation. It took eight hours to print out. Eventually I ended up with an Apple.

By then I was teaching at the graduate level and giving public speeches. I learned how to speak in public through teaching and learning from people I considered superb teachers. I would sit in on their classes to watch how they taught. I gave conference presentations at national and international meetings several times a year. If I was nervous before them, I would call my later beloved teacher, Baba Rexheb, and he would remind me of what King Solomon had on his ring—what was true for all situations. In Turkish it was *Bu da geçer*, "This too will pass." Baba would add one of the holy names of God after it. It made me relax and my presentations were well received. This was a far cry from the island Speech class. But in high school I had not seen the need or had any real models.

Finally though, there was important practical learning that we lacked on the island. We had no training in managing money. We did have a good economics class and excellent math classes, but nothing on the regular use of money for practical life. I did not know how to open a bank account or write a check when I went to college. I had no idea of budgeting or what my mother spent for food each week. I did not understand about savings, loans, taxes, investing, or interest. I had never heard of a credit score.

Part of the problem was people did not talk about money. This left young people in the dark. We needed to know about the cost of living. Yet if people never talked about it, how would we learn? We did not know enough to ask questions.

The only talk of money in my family came from my grandmother and my mother. My grandmother insisted that a woman should always have her own checking account. She always balanced hers to the penny. Her own father had lost his business several times and she was aware of financial matters. Later I understood that she meant that a wife should have her own account. Apparently many wives of her generation did not have their own accounts. As for my mother, she was "a child of the Depression." She even referred to herself this way. Detroit had suffered deeply in the Depression of the 1930s. Her father had lost all his money twice, and she was one of seven children. Her toes were not straight because she had not had shoes that fit. The lesson I took from this was to be afraid of debt. But neither my grandmother nor my mother gave me much substance for dealing with money.

The island had few commercial places, and there were not many ways to earn money, especially for girls. Most of us had stopped babysitting when we started dating. The boys could do some work like raking leaves and mowing lawns, or caddying at the golf courses. Still there were not regular jobs available.

And there was no Junior Achievement on the Island that could have helped young people learn about financial matters.

The summer after my freshman year in college my father told me I would go and live with my older sister in Ann Arbor and earn my keep. He said I needed to learn the value of money. He was right. I was totally naive about money. My sister lived in an apartment with two other young women. I could share her bedroom, but I needed to help pay the rent and cook one dinner a week.

So I went around Ann Arbor looking for jobs. Only my college in Vermont had let out later than the University of Michigan so many jobs were already taken. I ended up with three food service jobs—one for breakfast, one for lunch, and one for dinner. For breakfast I worked in a university dormitory. For lunch I worked in a French restaurant. I was not good there since they served alcohol and I did not know the names of drinks. When someone asked for a Harvey Wallbanger I thought they were joking. Throughout the late afternoon and evening I worked in a Greek pizza restaurant where I was wisely afraid of the Greek cook. My feet hurt by late night. I got a new respect for waitresses. And I learned how hard it is earn money in jobs like these, and how little is left over when the rent and expenses are paid.

I hope young people now have courses in personal finance. With cell phones and cars, they have higher expenses than we ever had. They need to understand credit cards and how important it is to pay them off on a monthly basis. College costs so much more, they need to understand about debt and loans early on. They must have jobs earlier too.

The Last Year of High School and "Finishing School" in Detroit

My father was a chemist, but when I had taken chemistry in eleventh grade I had not liked it. I told my father that no one could possibly be interested in heats of reaction. He differed with me on this. So when I went into twelfth grade, I was not excited to take physics—I assumed it would be like chemistry. My father told me that I needed physics to live in the modern world. In other words, I must take it. I wrote—"to live in the modern world"—in the front of my physics book. The first grading period I got a B+. But then I began to like it. I actually came to find physics fascinating. The questions were much more intriguing than those asked in chemistry, and I was glad my father had told me to take it.

Since my French was good, in eleventh grade I had been elected president of the French Club. One of the first things I did was eliminate parliamentary procedure. I figured it was not French. I went back to the French camp in Maine the summer after eleventh grade, so when I came into French class my senior year, I was fairly fluent in French. This caused a problem for the French teacher who was a fixture in the island school. She was from North Carolina and taught Spanish and French, both with the same North Carolina accent. The second day in class, she mispronounced the plural of "egg" in French and I corrected her without thinking. It is an irregular plural and a common mistake. There was silence in class. The next day in the morning I was told that I was officially expelled from French class for the entire year. I should go to study hall during the French period instead.

I told my parents about the situation. My mother had earlier found a war bride from French-speaking Belgium in Allen Park, a suburb of Detroit, for me to study with when there had been no French teacher. Now she would take over for my senior year too. My mother would drive me to study French with Madame Melling one day each week, the last hour of the school day. Madame Melling was from Liège and I think she was homesick. She had two daughters: Anne-Marie and Marianne. She loved the writing of Antoine de St. Exupéry. We read his works in French together, from *Le Petit Prince* (*The Little Prince*) and *Vol de Nuit* (*Night Flight*) to *Terre des Hommes* (*Wind, Sand and Stars*). She also had me memorize poetry, including a famous poem on the walled city of Carcasonne in southwest France which I still know. This was much better for me than the French class in the island high school, and probably saved the pride of the French teacher there too. I do not know how my mother had earlier found Madame Melling. She saved the year for me in French.

Meanwhile, we were the first senior class in the new high school that had been built not far from my old nursery school. My class seemed destined to always end up in new schools. So when Bill Rucker asked me out, it was in the hall upstairs of the new high school building by the walls of shiny new lockers. I was surprised. I had known him since kindergarten. The Ruckers were an old island family. I never knew he had even noticed me. We dated some. He was taller than me and attractive. I even met his parents and had dinner at his house on West River Road. But we did not have many interests in common.

That was the year that Grosse Ile did so well in football. Undefeated, 9-0 was our record, second in the state. Truly it was a remarkable year. We were also good in golf. There were several golf courses on the island and we had high school boys who were excellent golfers. I never learned how to play golf, nor did my mother. But my father was a golfer, and later my son learned on his own. What impresses me about golf is that, unlike football, it can be played throughout life.

In twelfth grade we had advanced placement English class with Mr. Appleyard. We read a book by John Ciardi called *How Does a Poem Mean*. What was good about it was not the literary theory so much as all the examples of excellent poems. Again we went to plays at the Hillberry Theater and the Bonstelle Theater in Detroit. Plays are meant to be experienced the way they were performed at these theaters.

In the fall many students were applying to colleges. My father had a business trip to the East and my mother and I went with him. We stopped along the way at different colleges that might work for me. My mother and I got lost at one point. We were trying to get to Mt. Holyoke and ended up on the wrong side of the river. So we ended up at Smith College instead and by chance there was a cancellation. Later I visited Mt. Holyoke but I liked Smith better. Every college I applied to accepted me. I had scored well on my SAT exams. Thanks to Mrs. Sells my math scores were even better than my verbal scores. And the idea of a girl from an island in Michigan was good for geographic distribution. I had asked Mr. Appleyard to write a letter of recommendation for me. Later I found out he had written that I was "a nice quiet girl." I had known he was lazy since he never had us write papers, but that is an especially dull recommendation. I guess other students had hyperbolic ones, so they needed "a nice quiet girl." I never thought of myself that way.

Unwisely I ended up going to a college we hadn't visited. My family had earlier gone to Montreal for the World's Fair and I had loved it. I had wanted to go to McGill University in Montreal, partly for the French spoken in Montreal. But my father said I had to go to college in my own country. So I went to Middlebury College in Vermont. It was the college closest to Montreal—not a good reason to choose a college. And it was known for languages. Little did I know that this reputation was mostly for its summer language school. I sometimes wondered what would have happened had I gone to Smith College. I think I would have liked it. But I ended up leaving Middlebury after two years and going to a better place for me, so it all worked out in the end.

My oldest friend Suzanne went to Wellesley College where she majored in chemistry. It was a good choice for her. Another friend, Leslie, went to Kalamazoo College, a very good Michigan college. She ended up going into the Peace Corps in Africa afterwards. Walt Wheeler went to the University of Michigan. It is an excellent university. Michiganders are fortunate to have it as a state university.

That year we had Mrs. Sawitsky for American history. She was a fixture in Grosse Ile high school and had taught there for many decades. She even got films from the Grosse Ile Naval Air Station on Vietnam for our class. I came home and told my father about "the domino theory" that I had learned from the films. He laughed in my face and told me what he thought of that idea. I did not mention this in class. When Mrs. Sawitsky was absent one week in the spring, we did not treat the substitute teacher well. He had us read aloud from the history textbook. We skipped pages at the end of each student's reading so nothing made sense. When Mrs. Sawitsky came back, she was aware that things had not gone well with the substitute. She knew we were seniors and were ready to move on. She made us behave by telling us that for those who would not go on to college these would be the last classes they would have.

A few weeks before the end of our senior year, we were told our class rank. Or at least the top students were since the top two had to give speeches at graduation. We had not been interested in class rank. When I got to college, my roommate from West Hartford, Connecticut, told me they had known their class rank throughout high school. That struck me as strange. My friend Suzanne was number one, and my other friend Leslie was number two. That meant Suzanne was valedictorian and Leslie was salutatorian. I was number three, and Walt was number four. I was relieved. The thought of giving a speech to an audience was awful to me. Little did I know that in the future I would spend my career speaking in front of university classes and giving talks at large conferences.

We had a class trip on a boat that went up north in Lake Huron and came back. I have vague memories of making out with a boy from another school whom I had just met and never saw again. We all came safely home.

We graduated, all 150 of us. As a class we were the largest ever to graduate—we had grown in size during high school with newcomers to the island. Most of us could not believe that school was over. We had been together so long — twelve or even thirteen years. Most but not all students went to college. A few students went to college outside Michigan like Suzanne and me. Some went to the University of Michigan in Ann Arbor. Others went to smaller colleges in Michigan. Many went to Michigan State University in the central part of the state. They would see each other and keep up relationships there.

The summer after my senior year I found a job picking strawberries. It was not easy to find jobs. But my family nixed it. Instead my grandmother sent me to a finishing school in Detroit—the John Robert Powers School. So I took the bus from Downriver up to Detroit four days a week, and then walked to Grand Circus Park to the Powers School which was on the second floor. I had no idea what "finishing school" involved.

It was a hot summer and I had to wear a dress every day and a girdle and nylons. I was skinny so the girdle did not make sense. I hated nylons. We were taught special ways of walking, including how to glide backwards across into theater seats without presenting "an unpleasant view," and how to hold both a drink and a cigarette. Since I did not smoke or drink this was useless. We were instructed in how to put on make-up, so much so that I did not wear make-up for many years. The only helpful part of make-up was how to trim eyebrows which I have used to this day. There were exercise classes. A young Black woman who was a member of the class and who owned several beauty salons told me under her breath in exercise class, "Frances, get in my way." She did not like the exercises and if I was in her way, she could not possibly do them. I was impressed with her entrepreneurial skills.

One interesting part for me was the scrapbook we had to make on fashion lines. I learned why the sari is the most attractive garment for all women and why beauty contestants all have diagonal sashes. Diagonals do not repeat any line in the human body.

For the last weeks of the class I stayed with my grandparents in Grosse Pointe on the east side of Detroit. My grandmother thought the finishing school would assist me in the future. She got tennis lessons for me too. I was not good in tennis. But I liked being with my grandparents. I would be going off to college. I would miss my grandfather and grandmother and they were getting older.

At the end of the summer it began to dawn on people from my high school class that for the first time we would not see each other in the fall. We would be going off to college. Before we had always been together. They and the island itself would stay with us in our memories for the rest of our lives.

The Toll Bridge connecting Michigan mainland to Grosse Ile. Photo by Greg Karmazin.

Epilogue

While we were still in college, the first tragedy struck. One island student from our class, Ron Solack, went to Wayne State University in Detroit where he played football with his friend Bill Cortis, another student from our class. During the fall of their junior year, after Ron had had an appendectomy the previous summer but was allowed to play football, he was kicked in the stomach on the field. It was at a game on Soldiers' Field in Chicago. He ended up at a hospital in Chicago. The team flew back to Detroit. But his friend Bill then drove back to Chicago since Ron was still in the hospital. Three weeks later Ron died of complications from surgery. He was not yet twenty. To have life cut down like this, from a sports injury, was unthinkable to us. No one wanted to believe it.

There would be other accidents that led to deaths as the years went by. Car accidents would take the lives of others from our class. Alcoholism would take some, and cancer would shorten others' lives. No one could predict how long people had or what lay ahead.

Most people moved away from the island, although a few stayed on the island, and some returned in later life. But we did come back for high school reunions. For the early reunions people checked out how others had done. But at the later reunions people relaxed, happy just to see each other and still be there. The island even began to feel somehow smaller, but it was still reassuring, with its bridges, its clear boundaries, and the river always flowing by.

We wondered if there was an essence to life on the island or an island mentality. The longer people lived there, it was natural that they would share ways of interacting. We mostly got along and were not competitive the way many in larger places were. We had a clear sense of place and we knew where we were from. We were proud of our island. People came back for our high school reunions for many years. I remember especially the fiftieth reunion.

Years later after my father retired, I asked him what he was proud of in his life. He told me that he was proud that he had kept the family in one place on the island. In his work in industrial chemistry to get ahead you were expected to move from company to company. He had had offers to move but had refused them all. Unlike his own boyhood where he had moved from Michigan to Arizona and then to a hospital in California for medical reasons, he wanted us to have a geographically stable growing up. He had provided that. I am most grateful to him for this. I would never have grown up on the island without my father's courage to refuse the business ways of success of the times. He had also stood up to his own mother who had wanted to send me to a boarding school so I would "meet the right people" to make a good marriage as she had.

Still when you grow up, you are changing through the years. It helps to have some constants. My family was there. Growing up on the island, even though it was changing too, provided more constants than many places in America in the 1950s and 1960s. It was a good place to grow up and a good place to be from.

There is a question as to how prepared young people were to go off-island for education and work. Families had responsibilities here. My parents encouraged independence and in my teenage years made sure I had several experiences off-island before college. Some of my classmates did not have this so going off to college was traumatic. It was the first time they had left the island. That is a danger if people get too used to the security and ways of the island.

The times also affected how prepared we were for life off-island. The 1960s were a time of opening up of Civil Rights. We did not have interactions with African Americans on the island. The late 1960s were a time of experimenting with drugs. A few islanders got caught in this trap, but not that many from my class. A fair number of us went on to professional careers.

There were divorces, and remarriages. But there were also several couples in our class who had met in high school and stayed married. The island culture was reticent about emotional life. If there was a drawback to growing up on the island, besides the lack of interaction with other races, then this was it. Reticence about emotional life may also be a feature of Midwestern culture, but I think it was amplified on the island.

At the same time, growing up on the island gave me a solid base from which to grow and observe. I remember sitting up high in the oak tree at age seven and vowing to get beyond Meridian Road. I did travel and work overseas in Turkey and Lebanon and in the Balkans. I also got to know different cultures: the Arab cultural community in Dearborn, Michigan; and the Albanian Bektashi community in metro Detroit. I worked with immigrants and refugees, and learned French, Turkish, Arabic, and Albanian. I loved teaching and research, and writing articles and books. I had a broad curiosity and desire to learn by doing and seeing and talking with people. Growing up in a small island community allowed me to relate to people from many other backgrounds without impinging on them. I was good at observing their ways. It helped that I had the contrast of my parents who had not grown up on the island. They also made efforts to introduce me to worlds beyond the island.

I always knew what home looked like for me and what it sounded like. I can see the shoreline out my window. I can recall the sound of the buoys and the foghorns. Home is always a wide river with Canada on the other side.

The Author

Frances Trix grew up on Grosse Ile from infancy through high school. To the surprise of her Midwestern family, at the university she majored in Turkish and subsequently traveled to Istanbul and later to Lebanon where she lived and taught, becoming fluent in Turkish and colloquial Arabic. She returned to the Detroit area where she worked in the large Arab immigrant community of Dearborn. She taught in the Dearborn Public Schools and then directed the Arabic-Bilingual program there. Throughout this time she continued to study in Turkish with Baba Rexheb, the leader of the Bektashi Sufi community outside Detroit. His community was made up of Albanians, so she learned Albanian and later studied and conducted research in the Balkans.

Frances completed a doctorate in Linguistics at the University of Michigan. She taught Anthropology at Wayne State University in Detroit for fifteen years, and Anthropology and Linguistics at Indiana University in Bloomington, Indiana, for ten years. She has published six books. Her most recent book is on host reception of refugees, based on her work in refugee transit camps in Macedonia and refugee programs in Germany. She retired to Detroit and lives on the river where she can see the Ambassador Bridge and across to Canada. Every morning she walks along the Detroit River.

BOOKS ON GROSSE ILE, CONSULTED

Corbett, Lucy and Sidney. *Pot Shots from a Grosse Ile Kitchen*. New York: Harper and Brothers, 1947.

— — —*Long Windows: Being More Pot Shots from a Grosse Ile Kitchen*. New York: Harper and Brothers Publishers, 1948.

Grosse Ile Historical Society. *Images of America: Grosse Ile*. Charleston, SC: Arcadia Publishing, 2007.

Keisel, Kenneth and the Grosse Ile Historical Society. *US Naval Air Station Grosse Ile*. Charleston, SC: Arcadia Publishing, 2011.

Keith, Julia J. *Our Little Island Grosse Ile*. Los Angeles: Harry T. Watson Printing Company, 1931; reissued by Grosse Ile Historical Society, 1962.

Swan, Isabella E. *Lisette*. Grosse Ile, Michigan: Isabella E. Swan, 1968.

— — —*The Deep Roots: History of Grosse Ile, Michigan, to July 4, 1876*. Grosse Ile, Michigan: Isabella E. Swan, 1976.

— — —*The Ark of God: History of the Episcopal Church, Grosse Ile, Michigan*. Grosse Ile, Michigan: Isabella E. Swan, 1977.

Woodward, Barbara and William Thomas. *Grosse Ile Then and Now: An Island Sketchbook and Tour Guide*. Prints by Wm. Woodward from the Ile Camera 1948-1953, Commentary by Barbara Woodward. Grosse Ile Historical Society, 2010 (updated).

OTHER BOOKS REFERRED TO IN THE TEXT

Carson, Rachel. *The Sea Around Us*. New York: Oxford University Press, 1951.

— — —*Silent Spring*. New York: Houghton Mifflin, 1962.

Catton, Bruce. *Michigan: A Bicentennial History*. New York: W.W. Norton & Company, Inc., 1976.

Holling, Clancy Holling. *Paddle-to-the-Sea*. Boston: Houghton Mifflin Company, 1941.

Miles, Tiya. *The Dawn of Detroit: Chronicle of Slavery and Freedom in the City of the Straits*. New York: The New Press, 2017.
Note: This book received positive national press when it came out. However I wish Miles had given more credit to local historian Isabella Swan for her much earlier biography of Lisette Denison that she published in 1965.

Trix, Frances. Glossary to Linguistic Terms, "Sugar Bush Speech of Detroit French Dialect," *French-Canadian Journal*, April, 1992.

Watts, Steven. *The People's Tycoon: Henry Ford and the American Century*. New York: Vintage Books, 2005.

Woodford, Frank B. and Albert Hyma. *Gabriel Richard: Frontier Ambassador*. Detroit: Wayne State University Press, 1958.

Acknowledgements

I have long wanted to write of growing up on Grosse Ile, an island in the Detroit River on the border with Canada. I cannot totally explain why. But when I finally had time, this is the part of my life that pulled my hands, as Yeats would say, to "bring the balloon of the mind" into the "narrow shed" of writing.

For historical references like early religion and churches on Grosse Ile, I want to give full credit to a local island historian, Isabella Swan, and her books on local history of Grosse Ile and the Detroit area. The main one is *The Deep Roots: A History of Grosse Ile Michigan to July 6, 1876*, published in 1976. Earlier she wrote *Lisette*, published in 1965, a biography of the former slave, Lisette Denison, who left much of her savings that led to the founding of St. James Church on Grosse Ile. For full references, see books on Grosse Ile and other sources at the end of this book.

Other than these references, my sources are my own memories. My oldest island friend, Dr. Suzanne Shanley Toce, kindly read the initial draft and gave me editing comments. My sister-in-law, Diane Trix, and brother, Herb Trix, read through the text. Herb caught editing errors. He also remembered certain events and teachers' trajectories that I did not. Erika Stevenson, a close friend who wrote her own memoir, read my memoir. My friend from the University of Michigan, Louise Myers, whose family were also Detroiters, also read the whole text. I spoke with Barry Dixon, and with Sheila Rogers DeMare and Frank DeMare, who went to Grosse Ile High School during my class years. Sheila and Frank have read the whole memoir and have given me valuable advice. I have tried not to write anything that would cause people embarrassment. I know that all islanders have their own memories of their growing up on the island, but I hope they will recognize similarities in what I recall as well. The island is a special place.